I0192294

NAVIGATE

Simplifying the Search for God's Will

Jason Creech

Published by
Innovo Publishing, LLC
www.innovopublishing.com
1-888-546-2111

innovo
PUBLISHING

Providing Full-Service Publishing Services for
Christian Authors, Artists & Organizations: Hardbacks, Paperbacks,
eBooks, Audiobooks, Music & Videos

All Scripture quotations, unless otherwise indicated, are taken from the Holy Bible:
New King James Version (NKJV), Copyright 1982.

New Spirit-Filled Life Bible, Copyright 2002 by Thomas Nelson, Inc.

Library of Congress Control Number 2012931594
ISBN 13: 978-1-936076-67-3
Cover Design: Jason Creech and Innovo Publishing
Interior Layout: Innovo Publishing, LLC

Printed in the United States of America
U.S. Printing History

First Edition: January 2012

SPECIAL THANKS

First and foremost, let me say how very thankful I am for our glorious God, His awesome Son, and the daily inspiration of the Holy Spirit. Words could never express how grateful I am for my mother and father. My parents have always encouraged my brother and me to dream and never give up. Thanks, Mom and Dad! There's not a week that goes by in which I don't think of how blessed I am to have Melissa as a wife. She's totally amazing! Sandra has been so kind to offer her gift of coaching and writing in several of my books—thanks, Sandra. Innovo Publishing is by far the greatest company in the world of publishing, and I'm very thankful for the team: Bart, Terry, and Darya, thanks for investing in me. I would like to thank each trailblazer for the added insight you brought to this project. Tori and Chaz, thank you for making parenting so much fun. I'm very proud of you both. Buster, thanks for all the good times and hard work you've shared with me. God is good!

Jason

THE GOAL OF THIS BOOK is to break through the ideologies that so often immobilize God's people. Hopefully, the examples of my stupidity will prevent you from falling into the same traps that held me captive during certain seasons of my Christian life. God created you with an intended purpose; live for nothing less. Everything He made was spoken into existence— everything, that is, except for you. When God made man, He got involved on a deeper level. On His hands and knees, He sculpted man's figure, and pressing His lips against Adam's, God breathed life into his lungs. When God made man, He got His hands dirty and His lips wet. Without a doubt, you are the workmanship of God, created in Christ for good works. You're a masterpiece! We all are. He spent more time making you and me than He did anything else He created. And no one wants you to discover the reason for your being here more than God does. You were not born to live and die without knowing why. I pray that my journey will help you through yours. God bless!

CONTENTS

IF IT'S GOD'S WILL, IT WILL HAPPEN

J ust because something is God's will, that doesn't mean it will come to pass. Think about it like this: the Bible says it is NOT God's will that "any should perish but that all would come to repentance" (John 3:15). However, people reject Christ and die lost every day. God's will does not always prevail over man's will. God gave us a free will, or in other words, the ability to choose whether or not we would obey His will. God's will for Adam and Eve was heaven on earth, but their will got in the way. Many times in my life, people have asked me to take a position or assume a responsibility that I knew was a part of God's plan for my life but at that time and under the circumstances, I wasn't at peace with the decision to do so. People around me would ask, "Don't you think God has called you to do this? Don't you think this is God's will for your life?" I've actually told people, "I believe this is a part of my future and yes, I do believe this is God's will for my life. However, I do not have the peace of God about this situation. Unless the circumstances change, I will not do it."

People will often use the "will of God" to manipulate those around them. Imagine going to a job interview and the first question the employer asks is, "Do you think this job is God's will for your life?" How would you answer that? How could you answer that, not knowing what the job responsibilities are, what the requirements are, and what the pay is? Church leaders use this question all the time. Many leaders believe this is a necessary step of faith for those entering a new position of ministry. Call it faith if you want, but blind faith is what gets possums killed crossing the roads at night. Actually, it's a subtle form of manipulation that hides behind the idea that real faith is making unwise decisions. Real faith comes when I know I'm getting paid less than what I hoped and doing more than what I imagined, but I do it anyway. I heard a story one time about a struggling church that found themselves in need of a pastor. While interviewing a young minister, the board chairman said, "We can pay you $25,000 this year, and $40,000 next year." The young man said, "Great! I'll take the job." The chairman asked, "When can you start?" The minister said, "This time next year."

Then you have those who believe if something is God's will, everything will work itself out. As if to say, "There will be no trouble along the way." That's like saying, "If it's God's will for me to go to work today, I'll start my car, pull onto the street, and when all the lights turn green between here and there, I'll go." That's crazy, right? Obstacles are a part of the journey. Trouble can be expected from time to time. Once, during a tough season of life, I got away to strengthen myself in the Lord. One week prior to my getaway, I woke up paralyzed on the right side of my face. The facial paralysis was just a drop in the bucket compared to everything else going on at the time. Looking for an encouraging passage, I turned to Psalm 91 and began to read out loud. Then I came to verse 15, "He shall call upon Me, and I will answer him; I will be with him in trouble . . ." For the first time I noticed that God didn't say He would keep me *from* trouble, but that He would be with me *in* trouble. Jesus said in John 16:33, "I've told you this so that my peace will be with you. In the world *you'll have* trouble . . ." (God's Word Translation). God's will is certainly not problem free—strong commitment is required. And commitment is when your hands and feet keep working when your head says, "There's no use!" Most people don't mind obstacles as long as they don't get in their way. Let's not forget; a kite works best against the wind, and the sweetest songs often come from broken hearts.

The Christian life is referred to as a "fight of faith." You can't have a fight without opposition. God gives us some wonderful advice in Ephesians 6:13–14, He says, ". . . and having done all to stand. Stand therefore . . ." Our job is to do all that we know to do and His job is to do the rest; only then can we rest assured that He who began a good work in us will perform it until the day of Christ (taken from Philippians 1:6). Be like a postage stamp and stick to it until you get there. A good friend of mine always says, "You got to hang in there like a hair in a biscuit." It's gross but true. If it's worth doing, it's worth enduring.

A PIONEER'S JOURNAL:

Psalm chapter ninety-one enumerates the encounters of a God explorer: terrors, danger, plagues, darkness, disasters, evil, death, lions, and serpents. In verses 14–16, God expresses His will concerning His explorers: "I will set him on high, I will answer him, I will be with him in trouble, I will deliver him, I will honor him, I will satisfy him, I will show him my salvation."

Reference verses 14–16. List the psalmist's three actions that initiated the "I wills" of God.

Which of these three actions need your attention?

SOMEWHERE BETWEEN AMBITION
AND EXHAUSTION

There's a certain level of ambition that accompanies the call of God on our lives. Call it ambition, drive, zeal, or passion. Regardless of what you call it, it's there and at times it can become a snare to us. Finding the balance between the ambition to do what God's called you to do, and the ambition to build your own platform can be quite tricky. Psalm 127:4 compares us to arrows in the hands of a mighty warrior. An arrow was created to penetrate a target. It was made to soar, to fly, to stop the fierce, to bring down the mighty. However, before an arrow can go forward, it has to be pulled backward. The further it's pulled away from its intended purpose, the more effective it is when it's released.

There are seasons in our lives when God pulls us from His quiver, places us upon His bow, and slowly begins to pull us back. These are very frustrating times. We're left confused. Seeing the target ahead, we wonder why we're not making progress. Every other word on our lips is, "Why." Someone once said that the two greatest days in our lives are the day we were born and the day we find out why. Discovering God's will for our lives is exciting; however, God often pulls us away from our destiny for a season. He does this in order to rid us of the selfish motives that are sure to ruin us. At some point, Satan's job to guard the throne of God turned into an ambition to build his own. His selfish ambition began his downfall. Prideful ambition turned a third of the angels into demons. God wants us to be more content being in His hand than doing what we do.

Let's look at Moses as an example. Acts 7 tells us that Moses knew he was called to lead God's people out of Egyptian bondage. When he saw an Egyptian soldier beating a Hebrew slave, he reacted violently. Assuming the time had come, Moses killed the soldier. Look at the biblical account of the story:

> And Moses was learned in all the wisdom of the Egyptians, and was mighty in words and deeds. Now when he was forty years old, it came into his heart to visit his brethren, the children of Israel. And seeing one of *them* suffer wrong, he defended and avenged him who was oppressed, and struck down the Egyptian. For he supposed that his brethren would have understood that God would deliver them by his hand, but they did not understand. And the next day he appeared to *two of* them as they were fighting, and *tried to* reconcile them, saying, "Men, you are brethren; why do you wrong one another?" But he who did his neighbor wrong pushed him away, saying, *"Who made you a ruler and a judge over us? Do you want to kill me as you did the Egyptian yesterday?"* Then, at this saying, Moses fled and became a dweller in the land of Midian, where he had two sons (Acts 7:22–29).

Forty years later, God visited Moses in the desert and spoke to him from a burning bush. What did God say? He said, "It's time, Moses. Go lead My people out of bondage." What did Moses say? He said, "No way, God. I'm not able. I can't do it. I don't have what it takes. Go call on someone more qualified. It won't work. I can't even talk plain." Something had happened to Moses during those forty years in the desert. He was a different man than before. Those lonely desert years had gutted him. He had been humbled, stripped of his deadly ambition to rule. I once heard a fiery preacher say, "You're not dangerous until you're dead!" Something in Moses had died, and that's where God wanted him. John the Baptist said, "He must increase, but I must decrease" (John 3:30). Paul said in Galatians 2:20, "I have been crucified with Christ and I no longer live, but Christ lives in me. The life I live in the body, I live by faith in the Son of God, who loved me and gave himself for me."

Have you ever been to a major theatrical production? During the Christmas season of 1995, I took my wife, Melissa, to see *The Nutcracker*. Later that night, I asked her to marry me. Now I'm not a sissy kind of guy, but the performance was pretty amazing. Though I'm not that crazy about men in tights dancing across the stage, outside of that it was really cool. But then, at the height of the act, everything stopped. A giant red curtain separated us from the excitement, the orchestra stopped playing, and everything came to a halt. It was intermission. The curtain call was made, intermission began, and it appeared as though the excitement was over. It's during these times that most people get up and walk out. But remember, there's always something happening behind the curtain. As a matter of fact, there's a lot happening behind the curtain. When the time comes, God will pull the veil open and everything will be new. Everything changes after the curtain call. The next time you seem to be at a standstill, just remember, He's creating something fresh behind the veil. It will be worth the wait.

Earlier this year, I had the privilege of meeting Hazem Farraj, host of the TV show, *Reflections*. Hazem is an incredibly talented lover of Jesus. He adds some wonderful insight into times of transition. Hazem wrote:

> I look back on my life and remember those awful times when the gruesome "hallway moments" seemed to get the best of me. What are hallway moments? Well, you've surely heard that age-old wisdom which says, "When one door closes, another one opens!" Or how about this one: "God has something better for you!" Now, I believe these nuggets of encouragement, and you'll find no objections here. However, there's fine print that's not mentioned! What do you do when you stand with that awful sound behind you, that sound of the door closing (if not slamming) and the loud insensitive horrible echo of the doorknob clinging to its place with echoes of fear reverberating into

the deepest core of your heart, which by the way, is beating so fast and hard as you stare into that dark hallway. You, my friend, are now officially in a hallway moment facing life's circumstances head on. There, you feel vulnerable, weak, and stripped of options, being exposed to an uncertain world of unknown with knocking knees and soaring blood pressure. Dramatic right? Well, first of all, relax. I have good news . . . this is normal and I will let you in on a secret that many people often cower away from.

You see, although these hallway moments in our lives may seem gruesome, the fact is that somewhere on the other side of that hallway, there is another door waiting to be opened! The art here is managing your composure in these rough times and having the wisdom to move or act in faith.

A PIONEER'S JOURNAL:

In Matthew 27:50, it took an earthquake to pull the veil apart to reveal God's Part Two—His plot to release His Presence into the world. This earthquake came as a result of Christ giving up His Spirit on the cross.

Are there things in your life that you have to "give up?" Name them.

Verse 52 states that when Jesus gave up His Spirit, the veil split. Simultaneously, many godly people who had died were brought back to life. As we offer our agendas and ambitions to God, life comes in other ways.

What areas of life might spring forth out of your personal "death" experience?

FROM ONE TRAILBLAZER TO ANOTHER
Obedience by Greg DeVries

When it comes to navigating through God's will for my life, I have come to realize that it is a daily process. The goal of this process is to follow Jesus. His instructions will always be, "If any man is going to follow, he must deny himself, pick up his cross, and follow Me" (Matthew 16:24; Mark 8:34; Luke 9:23). The emphasis tends to be on our self-denial. The apostle Paul declared he died not only a thousand deaths, but he died daily.

The greatest hindrance to the will of God for our lives is ourselves. The Spirit is willing and able to lead us and guide us into all truth. Yet still our flesh is contrary to the Spirit. Therein lies the need to die to ourselves. Even Jesus had to make such decisions when approaching the cross. "Not My will, but Your will be done" (Matthew 26:39). He learned obedience through the things He suffered.

As followers of Jesus, we need to embrace the situations that may be contrary to what we would desire for ourselves and surrender to His will. Notice the three middle letters of obe**die**nce. Living in the will of God will demand us to die to our own agendas. Obedience is simply doing what you are told to do, when you are told to do it, and doing it with the right heart attitude. Jesus was obedient unto death, even death on the cross (Philippians 2:8).

We lean in and take notice when someone teaches on the miracles preformed by Jesus. Signs and wonders were everywhere He went, and we should expect those things in our own lives as well. God is well pleased knowing we are His sons and daughters. It was at the baptism (representation of the old man dying) where God spoke to Jesus and all those around Him. "This is my son in whom I am well pleased." Jesus had yet to do anything supernatural and God was well pleased with Him as a son. So may our death to our flesh bring pleasure to God as well.

Notice the three middle letters of

obe**die**nce.

Living in the will of God
will demand us to die
to our own agendas.

MAN MAKES HIS PLANS BUT . . .

Years ago, I helped build some props for a drama our church performed. My job was to build the sacred Ark of the Covenant. To save money, I had to use some scrap lumber that lay behind the church. God only knows how long that half-rotted pile of wood had been there. Needless to say, my Ark was not as impressive as the one Indiana Jones discovered in his first movie. The assortment of wood consisted of a couple pieces of plywood and a few two by fours of various lengths. I cut the two longer boards the same length and did the same with two shorter pieces. Using my measuring tape, I marked the center of each board and made my cuts. The shorter boards made the width of the Ark and the longer made the length. I used this same random process to create the height.

After the production was over, someone asked me if I made the Ark according to the specs God gave to Moses. Now at the time, I only had a King James Version of the Bible, and in my Bible, God told Moses to build the Ark this many cubits high, this many cubits wide, and this many cubits long. I asked the guy, "How many inches equal a cubit?" The fella told me he had a study Bible that translated the measurements to inches. I almost passed out when he told me the dimensions. God told Moses to build the Ark exactly the same length, height, and width that I made mine. How crazy was that? I flopped down in a pew and pictured God laughing His head off. All my life, God has tried to show me, how "in the details" He really is. Proverbs 21:1 says, "The heart of the king is in the hand of the Lord and He will turn it wherever He wishes."

One verse that used to bug me to no end is Proverbs 16:9. The verse says, "A man's heart plans his way, but the Lord directs his steps." I'm a strategist—a planner. For years, I processed this verse as if God could care less about my plans. As if He was saying, "Go ahead and make your plans. Once the preparation is done, I will smash your idea and do what I want anyway." Later, I came to realize that God was not telling me to stop planning. He was only reminding me that it is His ultimate purpose that directs my steps. It is my responsibility to plan. It is God's responsibility to direct me through the planning process. Now when I sit down to strategize, I can thank Him for governing my decisions—even when they're made with uncertainty.

If I am encouraged to have the mind of Jesus, then I must believe that He is directing my thoughts. God told Adam to keep the Garden, but He didn't come down during the cool of the day with His hands on His hips, barking out orders like a nagging old lady—that was Eve's job! Adam was created with the skill and know-how to get the job done. The job was given to Adam to enjoy, not to stress over. *The Message* translation of Proverbs 18:18 says it best: "You may have to draw straws when faced with a tough decision." Sounds like something you'd find in a Chinese fortune cookie, doesn't it? But in the first chapter of Acts, we find the apostles doing just that.

After the death of Judas, someone was needed to take his place. Hundreds of years before the betrayal and death of Judas, King David predicted what would happen in great detail. According to the prophetic word, someone would be chosen to take Judas' place. So what did the apostles do? First, they established a certain criteria. The one chosen had to be an eyewitness of the life of Jesus beginning with the baptism of John until He was ascended into heaven after the resurrection. Two men were brought to the apostles: Justus and Matthias. Keep in mind we're not talking about electing a Sunday school superintendant. This person would have one of the greatest responsibilities in history. The Christian movement rested on the shoulders of these eleven men, and whoever was chosen would assume that same role. Considering what was at stake, how would one decide between the two? According to Acts 1:26, they cast lots, which to us would be about like playing a game of Go Fish. These eleven superspiritual-walked-with-Jesus guys rolled the dice, and the lot fell on Matthias. It was that easy!

When faced with an important decision, they did their best, and they trusted God with the rest.

A PIONEER'S JOURNAL:

Neither Justus nor Matthias are ever mentioned again in Scripture. Many theologians think that the Holy Spirit's choice for the twelfth disciple was the apostle Paul.

If this is true, how cool is it that God didn't rake them over the coals for their choice. In fact, it wasn't even mentioned.

What are some wrong choices that you regret making?

Do you believe God can redeem your wrong choices?

Make a faith declaration to grasp this truth by journaling your response.

STOP SEEKING GOD'S WILL

From the beginning of my journey with Christ, I've believed that God created me to preach the gospel to young people. Many times, I told people that I felt as though God had given me a word for a generation. I have been given the wonderful opportunity to work in a number of churches. As bad as I hate to admit it, while living in Alabama, I began to promote myself. I contacted national ministries and shared with them the call of God that was on my life. On a few occasions, I sent out flashy business cards and CD's of my best sermons. What an idiot! Looking back on those days is more than embarrassing; it's downright shameful. I had convinced myself that I was really only trying to reach a generation by pursuing the opportunities that would allow me to do so.

My wife and I moved our family to Atlanta to plant a new church. I was the student pastor, overseeing the children and youth ministries. Two years later, I left the position totally disgusted with what ministry had become. A friend of mine at the church knew that I was looking for work. He told me about a good friend of his who owned a high-end car dealership not far from where we lived. If I was interested, he promised to give his friend a call. A few days later, I walked into the showroom and asked to speak with the owner. A few minutes went by, then two men came walking toward me. One introduced himself as the owner. The other gentleman was a preacher friend of his. "Do you mind chatting with my friend while I wrap up some business," the owner said. Now I had never met either of these men before. They didn't know me from Adam.

But as the owner walked away, the man standing in front of me reached out to shake my hand and said, "You're about to make the biggest mistake of your life."

What a way to introduce yourself. How do you respond to that? He went on to say, "I see the fire of God in your eyes. You were born to preach to young people. I see you ministering to the hurting and broken and multitudes being saved." For one hour, this man read my mail. During my years of ministry, I've seen some far-out-there stuff, but I had never experienced anything quite like this. He said, "Your wife is struggling with fear, but she needs to remember that, I (the Lord), not you, am her provider. This call on your life is not a voluntary call, nor is it for a part-time position." Those words were crucial. We had been attending a fabulous church and days earlier, I had told Melissa that I would love to volunteer at the church and forget about full-time ministry. Over the months leading up to this event, I had become friends with a minister who led one of the largest youth ministries in the nation and he had just offered me a part-time job.

The car lot prophet then said, "At the end of the week, the Lord will reveal Himself to you. I also realize that you like living here in this area. However, you must be willing to go wherever He sends you, even if that means Memphis, Tennessee." Talk about details! Of course, I didn't become a car salesman that day, but the visit was more than worth it. When I got in my car, I started bawling. It was like I had spoken to God face to face. I don't even know what the guy's name was.

What I'm going to tell you next will be hard for you to believe, but with God as my witness—what I'm sharing with you is true. Seven days later, I was at my computer when the phone in my pocket started to ring. I didn't recognize the area code. "Hello," I answered. The fella on the other end said, "Is this Jason Creech?" "Yes," I said. He continued, "I pastor a church in Memphis, Tennessee, and I'm looking for a youth pastor. Last week I was talking to a worship leader in Florida and he said that I should give you a call. I'm going to be in Atlanta soon. Could we possibly get together while I'm in town?" I almost died. What on earth was happening here?

A couple weeks later, he and I met. He wanted someone to fill the vacant spot immediately but I was not that eager. Believe it or not, I did not have the peace of God about taking the assignment. It was as if God was trying to show me "how involved in the details" He was. A few weeks later, a pastor from Southeastern Kentucky called me about a job opening at their church. I had taken a job working for an apartment community, so he and I arranged to meet during one of my days off. Everything inside of me said, "Go." I will admit that I had a lot of questions; I grew up in Southeastern Kentucky, and it was the last place I wanted to be at that time. It proved, however, to be one of the best decisions we ever made.

Through these experiences, I have come to learn something about my journey with God. I don't have to seek His will. His will seeks me. All I need to seek is Him—His Presence. If I will delight myself in Him, He will give me the desires of my heart (Psalm 37:4). Those desires were placed there by Him anyway. My desires are a reflection of His will for my life. If God has called me, He will provide the platform for me in His timing. Oswald Chambers once said, "We are responsible for the depth of our character. God is responsible for the depth of our ministry."

A PIONEER'S JOURNAL:

Where's the self-promotion in the Scriptures?

Whose spot in Hebrews 11 came by the winning of a political campaign?

Maybe I'm being too harsh. I'm certainly not suggesting it's wrong to promote what we are doing. But don't forget; it was Samuel who found David, and it was Elijah who found Elisha, not the other way around. Jesus left us the greatest example. He did mind-blowing stuff, yet He forbade anyone to tell. He made Himself of no reputation.

WORKING ALL THINGS TO MY GOOD

It was the summer of 1995 and Melissa and I were both volunteering at a youth camp in Barbourville, Kentucky. As it turned out, we always ended up sitting across the table from each other during lunch every day. Camp began on Monday and lasted thru Friday evening. On Thursday, I remember telling a friend of mine that I was going to ask Melissa to go out with me the weekend after camp. I also remember him laughing his head off. You see, I was in my last year of college at the time, and Melissa had been a nurse for three years. To beat that, she was teaching at the university that I was attending! She's always looked much younger than she is, and I just assumed we were the same age.

Friday's lunch came and I sat down beside Melissa. To her right sat a guy who I thought was her brother; boy, was I wrong! It took me all week to build up the courage to ask her out, only to find out she was already dating someone. What an experience. As you can imagine, I was a little humiliated. However, as I was leaving camp that night, her older sister came over to me and said, "My sister is really interested in you. I think the situation she's in is about to change." There was hope after all. Now, this is embarrassing but it makes for a good story. The next week, I made a crazy home video asking her, once again, to accept my invitation to go on a date. A few days later, Melissa sent me a card in the mail expressing her appreciation. She said that she owed me a hug. A hug!

She never even said yes to the date invitation. In my mind, she was history.

A couple weeks went by and we had not seen or heard from

each other. Over and over, she watched that ridiculous video I had sent her. She told her dad, "I'm praying that if we're supposed to go out, I'll hear from him by this date," and with that, she threw a random date in the air. God must have marked that day on His calendar. A few days later, I received a call from the university. For some reason, my student loan check had arrived at the admissions office instead of my parents' house where I lived, which I will add was sixty miles away. On the same day, Melissa received a call from the same office. Her paycheck, which was always deposited directly into her checking account, was mysteriously printed and waiting for her in the admissions office. As fate would have it, Melissa and I met on the very day that she had petitioned God over—strange how He works. That December we were engaged, and by July of the following year, we were married.

Over and over again, God has proven to me how involved in my life He is. You see, when I was nineteen years old, I asked Jesus to be the Lord of my life. That was the best decision I've ever made. Psalm 23 says, "His goodness and mercy shall follow me all the days of my life." Romans 8:28 tells us that He is working all things together for our good. For this reason, I refuse to stress over God's will. I will make decisions, strategize and plan, and with complete assurance, I will trust that His will is being accomplished in me and through me. His will hunts for me. It chases me down. And because He is my God, He will finish what He started in me. Thanks be to God!

A PIONEER'S JOURNAL:

Proverbs 21:31 says, "The horse is prepared against the day of battle: but safety is of the LORD" (KJV). *The Message* Bible says it like this: "Do your best, prepare for the worst—then trust God to bring victory."

What is on your to-do list to prepare for your next adventure or assignment? List the first three things that come to mind.

Certain personality types are natural list makers who avoid risks, while others are spontaneous and revel in risk taking. Both types of people are strong in their own strengths and tendencies. Do you feel more comfortable making lists or diving in with spontaneity?

God deals with us individually. Many times, He will push us past our natural tendencies. He may tell the list maker to take the risk and the spontaneous person to make a list! What is He telling you?

DON'T BE AFRAID TO MISS GOD'S WILL

Once while Melissa and I were in the process of relocating, someone sternly warned me that if I got out of God's will, terrible things were sure to happen. A few days later someone else said, "I've never made a decision in life unless I was 100 percent sure it was God's will." Maybe that was why that person had lived in the same place for seventy years. It's just a thought. Nevertheless, I was scared half to death, and you know what happens when you get scared half to death twice!

Just the other day a friend of ours told us that her mother warned her saying, "If you get out of God's will, the devil will send you a man that you cannot resist. Before you know it, you'll be cheating on your husband and gambling away all your money." Wow! Where do we come up with stuff like that?

First of all, no one wants you to be in God's will more than God does. Secondly, no one can place you in His will any better than He can. Three times God audibly spoke to Jonah, telling him to go to Nineveh. Jonah was to warn the Ninevites of the wrath to come unless they turned from their evil ways. He knew what God wanted him to do, but he hated the people of that city. Despite God's clear command, Jonah boarded a ship and sailed in the opposite direction. While at sea, a storm threatened the lives of everyone on board. Jonah was thrown overboard. A giant fish swallowed the prophet. For three days, Jonah lived in its belly. It only took Jonah seventy-two hours to realize Nineveh wasn't that bad after all. At the end of the story, guess where we find Jonah?

In Nineveh. What was he doing? He was doing exactly what God told him to do in the first place.

Here's the question:

If Jonah knew God's will but deliberately rebelled, yet in the end found himself right in the middle of God's will, how much more can I rest assured that if I want to be in His will, He will see to it that I find myself there?

I know it's a run on sentence but I think you get the point.

The truth is, we seldom ever make a decision that we are 100 percent sure of. In Luke chapter one, an angel visited Zachariah in the temple. The purpose of the visit was to reveal God's will concerning the birth of John the Baptist. How did Zachariah respond? He asked, "How will I know for sure these things will come to pass?" Duh! You're looking at an angel, bonehead! Even in that undeniable circumstance, there was still some uncertainty. If we're not careful, we'll allow fear to paralyze us. The fear of missing God's will ironically keeps us from living His will. His will requires risks and uncertainties. Furthermore, I can't think of one great Bible character that didn't miss it at some point. Hebrews chapter eleven is full of Bible heroes that messed up terribly but still landed a spot in heaven's Hall of Fame. Don't let fear immobilize you. Go for it! You'll probably screw up a few times along the way, but God knew that before He created you, yet He made you anyway.

Someone once asked, "If you knew you would not fail, what would you attempt to do today?" The truth is, people never fail; they just give up. The only thing worse than a quitter is the man who is too afraid to begin. Removing fear from the equation can help us see clearly God's plan for our lives. Fear is perhaps one of the most overlooked sins. Part of me says, "Okay, but isn't there a healthy side of fear, like being afraid to walk outside during a lightning storm?" Sure, there's a respectful fear that we all need, but there's also a demonic element of fear that can hinder us from living in God's plan.

The Bible says that fear has torment, and anything that torments you is certainly not from God. Fear makes us believe the worst. There are 365 "fear nots" in the Bible—one for each day. Over and over God commands us not to be afraid. Sin is breaking one of God's commandments. When God says, "fear not," He's not giving us a suggestion, but a commandment. God says, "fear not" more than He says, "don't steal." He's serious about not allowing fear to dictate our choices.

When God said to Abraham, "Fear not," in Genesis 15:1, the Hebrew word for fear is *yare*, /*yaw-ray*/, which means "to be in reverence of something dreadful." It literally means to reverence or esteem something as higher than God. David did not fear Goliath because he esteemed God as mightier than his opponent. The giant was big, but he knew God was bigger. The first of the Ten Commandments is to have no other gods before the Lord. However, when I allow fear to keep me from doing what I hear God telling me to do, then I violate the first commandment. Furthermore, fear is also a lack of faith, and we know that without faith it's impossible to please God.

Please don't take this as a suggestion to not use common sense. However, God is in the business of stretching our faith. God works in the realm of the impossible. You can't say you trust God until you're facing the impossible. Every great achievement was once impossible. I love being around dreamers. One thing I've noticed about dreamers is they're driven more by passion than by particular circumstances. God created us to dream. He placed adventure in our hearts. Remember, wherever there's fear, there's opportunity, and the greater the fear, the greater the opportunity.

A PIONEER'S JOURNAL:

Fear is paralyzing. Most everyone has had a fearful dream in which you are unable to talk or move. This symbolizes what fear really does in our lives. It paralyzes us and keeps us from moving forward.

And almost always at the root of this kind of paralyzing fear is a lie that we believe about God.

At the root of fear are thoughts of loss—our reputation, our relationships, our position. It is said that fear of loss is an indication that we have transferred our dependence from God upon the thing we fear losing.

What are you afraid of losing?

What misconception about God are you believing?

TOTALLY DEPENDING ON GOD

In March of 1992, I became a Christian. Well, sometimes I think I'm part Christian and part heathen—today I'm about 60/40. Over the years, I've met many wonderful believers who for some reason or another have a difficult time making important decisions. Some have shared with me their fear of missing God's will. Immobilized by their anxiety, they "wait on God" to reveal to them what they should do. If God doesn't speak, they don't do anything. Now let me clarify something before I go any further: there are times when the Holy Spirit prompts us to do (or not to do) something. We read in Acts 16 that Paul wanted to preach the gospel in Asia and Bithynia, but the Holy Spirit would not allow him to do so. God does give clear directions at times, but certainly not all the time.

When it comes to making important decisions in life, many folks hide behind an attitude of "totally depending on God." The ironic thing is, if God told us everything He wanted us to do, how to do it, and when, then we wouldn't need to trust Him. Real faith is displayed when I take a step that I'm not sure of. Real faith is required when I make a difficult decision not knowing how things will turn out. As difficult as this might sound, "God never tells us everything." When God appeared to Moses in the burning bush, He told Moses to go lead Israel out of Egyptian bondage. God did not tell him all the trouble he would go through along the way. If God had told him everything, Moses would have thrown a bucket of water on that blazing bush and walked away! Think about the difficulties Moses faced in his obedience to God's will:

- Pharaoh made the Hebrew slaves work harder and under harsher conditions—Exodus 5:4–21.
- God's people did not believe that the Lord had sent Moses—Exodus 6:9.
- The Israelites feared for their lives at the Red Sea—Exodus 14:10–12.
- They nearly died of dehydration in the wilderness—Exodus 15:22–24.
- Three thousand people were killed because of idol worship—Exodus 32:27–28.
- The people were plagued for their rebellion—Exodus 32:35.
- Because of Israel's complaining, the Lord set fire to their camp—Numbers 11.
- The weight of Moses' responsibility became too heavy for him—Numbers 11:11.
- Repeatedly, the people would despise Moses for leading them out of Egypt—Exodus 15:24, 16:2, 17:3; Numbers 14:2, 14:36, 16:41, 20:2, 21:5, and 26:9.
- Many of Israel's strongest men died when God gave them the meat they craved—Numbers 31–35 and Psalm 78:26–32.
- Moses' sister, Miriam, and Aaron, his brother, criticized him behind his back and stirred up a revolt against him—Numbers 12:1.
- Regardless of the many astounding miracles that God did for His people, they refused to enter into the Promised Land for fear of the inhabitants—Numbers 13:14.
- Due to their fear and unbelief, a death sentence was pronounced upon everyone twenty years old and older with the exception of Caleb and Joshua. Moses had to lead them through the desert for forty years until those older generations died away—Number 14:26–33.
- Korah, Dathan, and Abiram led a rebellion against Moses and Aaron. The ground opened up and swallowed them and their families, and fire consumed 250 people. Many of the people blamed Moses and Aaron, so the Lord sent a plague and 14,700 fell dead—Numbers 16.
- Fiery serpents bit and killed many because they spoke

against God and Moses—Numbers 21.

- Twenty-four thousand died because of their harlotry in Moab—Numbers 25.
- Psalm 106 recalls a list of Israel's stubbornness as Moses led them from captivity to the land of promise.
- And let's not forget that before Moses even reached Egypt, the Lord nearly killed him because he had not circumcised his son—Exodus 4:24–26. That's hitting below the belt—literally!

Despite the fact that Moses put up with all their garbage, God would not allow him to enter the Promised Land because he struck a rock twice when he was told to strike it only once. Now, what on earth is that all about? Talk about some injustice! You see, God left out all those minor, or should I say, "major" details. He never tells us everything. If He did, our lives would never require faith.

Think about the miracle of turning water into wine. Mary told the servants, "Whatever Jesus tells you to do—do it." Jesus told them to fill six water pots "with water," then take what they had in the pots to the host of the party.

That's all the instructions He gave.

That's all He said.

But they obeyed and somewhere along the way, the water became wine. You see, obedience is the conduit through which miracles flow. A man once asked his radical Christian friend, "If God told you to jump through a wall, would you do it?" The friend said, "Yes, sir. It would be my responsibility to jump, and God's responsibility to make a hole."

A PIONEER'S JOURNAL:

There is a scene in *Indiana Jones and the Raiders of the Lost Ark* where Jones has found the Ark. However, the Ark is on the other side of a large chasm—an abyss. There is absolutely no way to get to the Ark. With the Nazis closing in behind, Jones steps out into the air. A stepping stone appears! He takes another step and another stone appears. He continues until he reaches the other side to rescue the Ark. The stepping stones do not appear until he takes the step!

Steven Spielberg must have read Joshua's account in Joshua 3:14–17 . . .

> So the people left their camp to cross the Jordan, and the priests who were carrying the Ark of the Covenant went ahead of them. It was the harvest season, and the Jordan was overflowing its banks. But as soon as the feet of the priests who were carrying the Ark touched the water at the river's edge, the water above that point began backing up a great distance away at a town called Adam, which is near Zarethan. And the water below that point flowed on to the Dead Sea until the riverbed was dry. Then all the people crossed over near the town of Jericho. Meanwhile, the priests who were carrying the Ark of the Lord's Covenant stood on dry ground in the middle of the riverbed as the people passed by. They waited there until the whole nation of Israel had crossed the Jordan on dry ground.

What would have happened had the priests waited for the water to abate before taking the first step?

What abyss separates you from your passion, your prize?

What are you waiting on?

JUST RELAX

A few months after I became a Christian, our youth group attended a revival. Before the service started, the evangelist was playing softly on the keys. I closed my eyes and began to drift off in worship. Out of nowhere, I envisioned myself standing before the student body of a public school. I was sharing what Jesus Christ had done in my life. A team of youth was with me. They were each a part of the production; some danced, a few played instruments, and others sang. The students in the bleachers began weeping. Hundreds poured out of the stands asking for prayer. With everything in me, I believed that God was showing me a glimpse of my destiny, and I was pumped!

When the service was over, I shared what I saw with my youth pastor and his wife. "What should I do?" I asked. He said, "If it's God, it will happen." That's a nice way of saying, "I think you're stupid, but I don't want to hurt your feelings." A few weeks later, I called the 700 Club prayer line and shared my experience with a sweet old lady who agreed to keep me in her prayers. She thought I was nuts too.

It was 1992 when all that took place. In 2006, I was doing a teaching series during our Wednesday night high-school services, and a local principal had sneaked in the back door to listen. The next day he called and asked if I would come to his school and share a word with his students. Two weeks later, another school called. Within a few months, I was speaking in schools two or three days a week. At the close of the year, I had spoken to roughly 10,000 students. During this time, I was invited to speak at an annual conference for public school administrators. This led to more speaking engagements. Soon I had spoken to over 54,000 students, booking events as much as a year in advance. A team of youth traveled with me as well. Over fifty dancers worked on a rotation, and just as I had envisioned, several played instruments and a few sang. At one point, nearly two hundred volunteers assisted in some form or fashion.

The Holy Spirit began dealing with me in a very unusual way. It was as if He wanted to speak to me but I heard nothing. A couple weeks later, I loaded my camping gear, my Bible, notebook, and pencil, and off to the woods I went. The next morning I walked to the edge of the woods and said, "Lord, I'm not going to stop walking until you speak to me."

You should never say things like that to God.

Three hours later, I heard a gunshot and realized that I had picked the opening day of deer season to venture deep into the woods. I hit the ground and said, "Speak to me, Jesus!"

God did speak to my heart that day. The Lord challenged me to start an event called The Becoming. My new assignment would be to help students in our area go to college for free to become all God created them to be. It sounded good, (and there was much more to it than that) but as excited as I was, I had no idea how it was going to work. The next day I spoke with a friend of mine who worked for a local community college. I knew she had a lot of pull with the college president, and I was sure she could help. At first she seemed optimistic, but two weeks later she said it wouldn't work.

Several months went by and I was asked to speak at a conference on a college campus. At the end of my session, I took five minutes and shared my dream of The Becoming. After I dismissed the crowd, a lady came to the front and handed me a business card. She said, "That's my dad's card. He's the dean of a college not too far from here, and I think he would be interested in hearing about your endeavor." Three years later, we had sent thirty-three young people to college for four years—for free! The total cost of their education was $125,000 per student. All they had to pay for was books. Over $4 million in scholarships were given away during those three years. Hundreds of young people were saved during our evening events. A few days after one of our productions, a young lady who attended was killed in a car wreck. She had filled out a salvation card at the event. After the accident, I looked at her card, and noticed the first half of her e-mail address was SmilingAngel@... God is so good.

Habakkuk 2:2–3 says, "Write the vision and make it plain on tablets, that he may run who reads it. For the vision is yet for an appointed time; but at the end it will speak, and it will not lie. Though it tarries, wait for it; because it will surely come . . ." There's an appointed time for each dream God births in your heart. Let the words of Habakkuk be an encouragement to you. Write down the vision, make it simple, do what's necessary, and in time, it will come to pass.

Through this journey of one blunder after another, I've slowly come to realize that God must know what He's doing. I don't know what your life is like right now, but one thing I'm sure of is that God has an amazing adventure waiting for you. Don't stress out wondering about the details; just relax and enjoy Him. It's His work; let Him figure it out.

A PIONEER'S JOURNAL:

Habakkuk 2:2 says to write the vision and make it plain on tablets.

Once you write something in large letters on tablets of stone, you've pretty much "written it in stone." It's kind of hard to take it back. You are committed.

After you've written it in stone, Habakkuk 2:3 says to wait for it. *Strong's Exhaustive Concordance* says this word *wait* means "to adhere to or to tarry" and comes from a root word meaning "to carve out, to intrench."

What is your "write it in stone" moment?

What mental picture comes to you as you think of carving out a place to wait on and adhere to God?

FROM ONE TRAILBLAZER TO ANOTHER

Breathe Easy by Harry Saylor

I doubt if there is anything more intriguing than determining the "will of God" for your life. After all, is there anything more important than that? For most, it's like looking for a needle in a haystack. But I have to ask myself, "Is our God toying with us in some kind of cat-and-mouse scenario in order to catch us in some kind of life-threatening situation?"

As I began to think in my own life about discovering the "will of God," I had an epiphany moment. I realized that it was not my finding the will of God as much as it was the will of God finding me. The two most important decisions in my life—the woman I would marry and the place I would serve within the Kingdom, which were both out of my own known realms—were brought to me through people who had no idea of the magnitude of their participation. So with that in mind, I began to rethink about the men and women of the Bible. The first person I thought of was Abraham. He wasn't looking for the will of God. God found him. The more I looked, it became evident from David, Esther, and all the way to the twelve Jesus chose, the will of God found them. Even the apostle Paul, on his way in the wrong direction, was arrested by the will of God.

Romans 12:2 in the NLT says, ". . . let God transform you into a new person by changing the way you think. Then you will learn to know God's will for you, which is good and pleasing and perfect." I dare say there are many who are a bit apprehensive about doing God's will out of some strange sense that it's going to force them to do something they wouldn't like. What if you began to think the Scripture I just quoted was true and all God had in mind for you was good, pleasing, and perfect? Not only that, but God is revealing His will to you and not withholding it from you. I am convinced that His will, will find you!

Even the apostle Paul,
on his way in the wrong direction,
was arrested by the will of God.

A CHANGE OF PLANS

Does God change His mind? Could God ask me to do something one minute then something different the next? What if God gave me a specific order, but before I finished, He changed things up on me? Is it possible that what God told me to do today might change before I reach tomorrow? These are some questions I've struggled with during my journey with Jesus. Several times in my life, I've been so sure God had spoken to me about doing something. Without a doubt, I knew it would happen. Then to my surprise, things changed. All of a sudden, what was so clear became foggy with uncertainty and bewilderment.

During one of these seasons in my life, someone asked me this question: "Are you doing what God said, or are you doing what God is saying?" If Abraham had done what God said, he would have offered Isaac as a burnt offering. Because Abraham kept his ear open to God's voice, he heard the Angel of the Lord say, "Abraham, Abraham! Do not lay your hand on the lad" (Genesis 22:11–12). Nine verses earlier, God told Abraham to offer his son on the mountain; now God was saying, "No, don't!" Does God change His mind?

In 2 Kings 20, God told the prophet Isaiah to tell King Hezekiah he needed to settle his affairs quickly because he would soon die. Before the prophet could get out the door, God told him to go back and tell the king that he would live fifteen more years. Was God giving the prophet mixed signals? Before Herod began killing all the male children, an angel appeared to Joseph in a dream and told him to take Mary and Jesus and flee to Egypt. In Matthew 2:19, the Bible says that after Herod died, an angel again appeared to Joseph and told him to return with his family to Israel. Two verses later, we read the following:

"But when he heard that Archelaus was reigning over Judea instead of his father Herod, he was afraid to go there. And being warned by God in a dream, he turned aside into the region of Galilee."

Now wait just a minute! Did you catch that? God told Joseph to do one thing, but as he was doing what God told him to do, God told him to do something different. Malachi 3:6 says, "I am the Lord, I do not change . . ." So what can one make of all this?

Simple.

God doesn't change, and neither does His plan, but the details . . . they're not set in stone. It was always God's will for a sacrifice to be made on Mount Moriah, just not Isaac. King Hezekiah was going to die, just not right away. Joseph . . . your guess is as good as mine.

Things change for a number of reasons. In Hezekiah's case, it was the king's prayer that altered the timing of his death. The unbelief of the children of Israel kept them from entering the Promised Land at the time God intended. Achan's sin kept Joshua and his men from defeating the small city of Ai. God had promised Joshua that no man would be able to stand before him all the days of his life, (Joshua 1:5). Jericho was a testimony of God's faithfulness to honor His Word; however, Achan's actions changed things. Often, God's will is contingent upon our willingness to obey. Because Achan disobeyed God, thirty-six men died and Israel suffered a major defeat. God may tell you that it's His will for me to give you $1,000, and perhaps it is, but in order for His will to become a reality, I must be obedient.

Brad Freeman, a good friend of mine, once shared with me a teaching he did titled, *Three Reasons to Kill Isaac*. His insight could not have come at a more needed time. I was definitely living in the land of confusion. Six months prior, I knew without a doubt what the Lord was telling me to do. His will was confirmed to me over and over again. I stepped out in obedience and things were moving forward. But then something odd began to happen. Something inside of me didn't feel right. There was no longer any joy, and the peace of God had left. I had never experienced anything like that in my life. Then Brad came along . . .

Three Reasons to Kill Isaac:

1. Because God told me to. What better reason is there than that?
2. We've come too far to turn back. Put yourself in Abraham's shoes for a minute. He had assembled a team, servants, equipment, and mules. They invested time and resources. Much had been done in order to do what God commanded. When you've gone to that extreme, it's not easy to change directions. What happens to the momentum? Will the people take him seriously the next time he claims that God has spoken to him? When the team doesn't accomplish an objective, it does something to the morale.
3. What will people say when I return home and Isaac is with me?

So what about it? Can God ask you to do one thing one minute and change directions the next? Does God change? No. And neither does His plan, but the details . . . they're not set in stone. Keep your ears open!

A PIONEER'S JOURNAL:

Has God ever thrown you a curve ball?

What happened?

How did you deal with it?

Looking back, would you have done anything differently during that time, and if so, what?

What are you thinking after reading this chapter?

How does this impact your outlook on God's will?

WHAT DO YOU WANT TO DO TODAY?

A few days ago, a friend of mine, Joe Farmer, was sharing a thought with me concerning God's will. Joe said one of his favorite moments each week is when he wakes up the kids on Saturday morning. While they're lying still and quiet, he jumps onto the bed, begins tickling them without mercy, and then he asks, "What do you want to do today?" I can so relate to that picture because I do and say the same thing every Saturday.

I sneak in the room,

Peer over my kids' still bodies,

Watch them breathe . . .

Then pounce on them like a lion.

Stick my fingers in their ribs.

Give them a second to breathe again.

Then ask the question, "What do you guys want to do today?"

It happens at my house every Saturday morning, and I love it. Joe said as he woke his children a few weeks ago, he got this overwhelming thought concerning God's will. He said that most of his Christian life he's repeatedly asked God the question, "What do you want me to do?" Have you ever asked God that question? I know I have. At times, it torments me that I don't hear God's reply. But Joe said, "Could it be that God does to me, what I do to my kids on Saturday morning?" If God is our Heavenly Father, and we know He is, then how often does He peer over our beds in the morning, smiling as we breathe, tickling us just enough to wake us without scaring the poop out of us, and when we open our eyes, He asks, "What do you want to do today?"

Not, "Here's your to-do list for the day."

Not, "You didn't finish your chores yesterday, so that just means more work today."

No, but on the contrary, "What do you want to do today?

What are you dreaming of today?

What would you like to dare to do today?"

You see, I've come to realize that the dreams I carry in my heart—God put them there. My passion, drive, ambition—God instilled those things in me. God's called us to dream, to order our day, to make decisions, and to dare. More importantly, He says, "Let's do it! I'm with you. This will be fun!" In his book, *Free Book*, author Brian Tome[1*] says, "God didn't start things on earth with an iron fist. He started with amazing gifts, ownership, and the okay to make big decisions. He doesn't want followers who are bogged down by anxiety. He wants imaginative, fulfilled, and dynamic followers who are running right alongside Him."

So, let me ask you the question, "What do you want to do today?" Seriously! Think about it. Write it down.

---

[1] Brian Tome, *Free Book* (Thomas Nelson Publishing, 2010) p. 17.

A PIONEER'S JOURNAL:

When seeking God's will, ask yourself: What am I most passionate about?

Where are my giftings?

In what areas am I presented with the most opportunities?

Answering these questions will point you right toward your God-given purpose.

SILENCE—THE IMPORTANCE
OF BEING STILL

In 2007, Will Smith starred in the apocalyptic movie, *I Am Legend*. What appeared to be a miracle cure for cancer ended up killing 90 percent of the world's population.; only a remnant survived. Most of the survivors displayed wild, animalistic behavior. For years, Smith's character feared that he was the only human immune to the outbreak and the last sane person on the planet. He was wrong. Smith met a woman who claimed God revealed to her the location of a survival colony. This sent Smith into a rave of atheistic sarcasm. Taunting her claim, he questioned, "God spoke to you?" I love her response. She said, "Yes, God spoke to me. The earth is quiet now, and we can hear His voice again."

Doctors now have a term used to describe the excessive amounts of noise that fills our ears these days. Many cities across the country have passed legislation to protect its citizens from noise pollution. Noise pollution? For most of us, we seldom use those two words side by side. However, there's a growing concern for our lack of serenity. In New Haven, Connecticut, if the folks next door interrupt your "quite enjoyment," a lawsuit can be filed against them. According to the city's noise ordinance law, when a noisy neighbor's intrusion on your peace is consistent and the noise is excessive, you may have a valid claim for damages.

In high school, my dad helped me install a kickin', heart-pounding, ear-bleeding, car stereo system. CDs were fresh on the market, and I was first in line to get one. Giving voice to my new MC Hammer CD was two 1,000-watt 15-inch subwoofers, two 120-

watt 6x9's, two 200-watt 10-inch subs, and two tweeters. Powering all that was my open-air display of amplifiers resting on top of the giant box that covered the area where my backseat used to be. It's a wonder every bolt in my car didn't back out as I drove down the highway. Perhaps there's a connection between my kickin', heart-pounding, ear-bleeding, car stereo system and my inability to hear Melissa telling me to take out the trash.

A blog post from see-the-sea.org raises a few interesting thoughts concerning our noisy planet:

> From the beginning of time, the oceans have been filled with sounds from natural sources such as the squeaks, moans, and clicks of whales and dolphins, the snapping of shrimp, the sound caused by wind upon the surface. The ocean's marine species have their own specialized acute hearing, communication skills, and echolocation abilities at natural sound levels. Hearing is generally as important to many marine creatures as sight is for humans.
>
> The ocean, once referred to as "The Silent World" by Jacques Cousteau, has now become an increasingly noisy place since the industrial age. It is estimated that the ambient ocean noise has increased ten decibels (ten times increase in sound) between 1950 and 1975.
>
> An increase in motorboats, commercial shipping traffic, exploration, extraction of oil, sonar, and even coastal jet ski traffic is contributing to the increased level of underwater noise. "If you could lie down under the shipping lanes at Great South Channel (off Cape Cod) and spend the day there, you would get the impression of being on the tarmac at Logan Airport," said Christopher W. Clark, who runs the Bioacoustics Research Program at Cornell University.
>
> Sound travels four times faster in water because water molecules are packed tighter together. High intensity sound in the oceans can

travel for thousands of miles. In this regard, it is important to remember that since water has a much greater density than does air that sound waves travel though water at much higher energy levels and are hence louder.

We know that whales and dolphins use sound to communicate with each other over vast distances. Other marine species use sound to find food and choose mates as well as warn others of potential dangers. Whales communicate at very low frequencies, below 1000 Hertz. This is the same frequency that resonates from many human-caused activities. Man-made sounds are drowning out the calls of mates, calves, and other pods that these mammals depend on. High sound levels cause grey whales to deviate from their migration paths, the deviation being greater as sound intensity increases.

More recently, new sources of marine sound pollution have been added to the mix. The one source having the most immediate and obvious negative effect has been the development and subsequent testing of "Low-frequency Active (LFA) Sonar" with a potential worldwide deployment by the U.S. Navy and NATO. There have been several tests that have directly resulted in large losses in marine life.

During March of 2000, at least 17 whales stranded themselves in the Bahamas and the population of Beaked Whales in this region disappeared. A federal investigation identified testing of a U.S. Navy active sonar system as the cause. According to an article posted by the Natural Resources Defense Council, "More than a dozen harbor porpoises were found dead on the beach near the San Juan Islands soon after the Navy tested active sonar in the Haro Strait in May.

Over time, we have slowly turned the volume of this world up until we've almost completely lost our ability to hear the most important sound we could possibly hear—the sound of God's voice. The Bible says that God speaks with a still, small voice. God whispers. He speaks softly. You have to be still, quiet, and close to hear a whisper. Whispers aren't heard by accident; they're heard intentionally. If we're going to hear the voice of God, we have to be intentional about it. We have to silence everything around us, draw close, and listen.

As a kid, I remember being scared to death by the noises my house would make during the night. Everyone in my family seemed to fall asleep as soon as their head hit the pillow. I, on the other hand . . . well, I was always looking straight up with both eyes wide open. For the life of me, I couldn't figure out why our house made so much racket.

Pops.

Crackling sounds.

Squeaky noises.

It was like our nice yellow farmhouse would wait all day for me to lie down, and then every board, screw, pipe, and shingle worked together as an orchestra, chiming what could have easily been the sound track for *Nightmare on Elm Street*.

Well, as I got older, I realized that my house wasn't waiting on me to go to sleep to make noises; it had been making noises all day long. I just wasn't quiet enough or still enough to hear it. In the same way, God is always speaking. We're not always listening. Several times in the New Testament God spoke in an audible voice, but those present thought it was only thunder.

Jesus said, "I don't speak My own words, I speak what I hear the Father say" (John 12:49–50, 5:19, 8:28, 8:38, and 15:15). Jesus said that when the Holy Spirit comes He will not speak on His own authority, and He will only speak what He hears (John 16:13). Genesis 15 says, ". . . and the word of the Lord came to Abraham . . ." 1 Samuel 15 says, ". . . and the word of the Lord came to Samuel . . ." 1 Kings 13 says, ". . . now it came to pass as they were eating that the word of the Lord came to the prophet . . ." The Bible is filled with these examples. God spoke then, and God is still speaking now. If we will get still enough and quiet enough, we can hear what He has to say. In Matthew 11:15, Jesus said, "Let those who have ears use them to listen!" (New Century Version). Jesus often used phrases like this to heighten an awareness to the reality of God's voice.

Think about the noise around you. When you're in the vehicle by yourself, do you turn on the stereo? Do you fill up that alone time with phone calls? When's the last time you drove in silence? When you're at home, do you always have the TV playing in the background? Just the other day, I was driving down the road and my son was in the back seat playing his new video game. Right in front of us appeared the strangest rainbow I've ever seen. I started yelling, "Chaz, look at that rainbow! Look! Look! Look!" Frustrated at my command to look, he shouted, "I'm about to go to another level, Dad! I can't look right now!" How crazy is that? God's doing wild things all around us, but we're too busy playing with gadgets. Turn it all off. Tune it all out. Start listening.

Have you ever been talking to someone and the entire time they're distracted by something? They're standing right in front of you but they're looking around you, and you know they're not "tuned in." How do you think God feels when we're always distracted by something other than what He's saying?

Let's try something, spend the next ten minutes in silence. Take out a blank piece of paper and begin writing down every sound you hear. Don't miss anything—the clock ticking, the fan blowing, that car driving by, everything—write them all down.

Begin now.

Take some time out of each day, and sit quietly. Begin by asking the Lord to draw you close to His side. Tell Him how excited you are to hear what's on His heart. As you listen, write down the spontaneous thoughts that race through your mind. Every thought, write it down. Thank the Holy Spirit for giving you the mind of Christ. Be like Joshua who, when encountering the Lord said, "Speak, Lord, for your servant listens."

I'm not asking you to do something I've not practiced in my own life. For several years, I went to my place of prayer around 4:30 a.m. My work day didn't start until 8:00 a.m. so that gave me plenty of time to pour my heart out before God. On the first Friday of each month, I would meet with a few friends at a church and pray from 11:00 p.m. until 6:00 a.m. the next morning. On one-hour intervals, we would worship, repent for the sins of our nation, intercede, ask God to do in us what only He could do, and off and on, we would sit quietly and listen. At least twice a year, I would go stay in a cabin for the weekend to fast and pray. Some of the most powerful encounters I've ever had with the Lord came during those times.

As a leader, I realize that ministry begins with hearing God's voice.

"Jonah, go to Nineveh."

"Moses, go tell Pharaoh to let My people go."

"Paul, take the gospel to the Gentile world."

First the instruction, then the action.

Instead, we tend to act first, then ask God to bless the action.

In John 10:27, we read where Jesus likens us to sheep. As our shepherd, we hear His voice and act on what we've heard. Hearing from God gives me the confidence I need to stand against whatever comes my way. It also empowers me to cast vision and recruit volunteers. I want to be a listening leader with ears finely tuned to the sound of His voice.

A PIONEER'S JOURNAL:

Some people are afraid of the quiet. They are afraid of what God might ask them to do.

How about you?

Is there a connection between the noise in our lives and our inability to hear God's voice?

FROM ONE TRAILBLAZER TO ANOTHER
Hearing God in Critical Times by Rick Clendenon

Years ago, I read a great book by Bob Buford entitled *Halftime*. The title is self-explanatory, revealing that ministry is seasonal, filled with transition, and we must remember that we cannot play every season the same way, especially if we expect to win.

My personal halftime arrived in 1991. After eighteen years of active ministry, I suddenly found myself alone with my family, back in my hometown, without an assignment, feeling like a failure, and wondering if I knew how to hear from God at all. Little did I realize that it was just halftime, for my most productive years yet lay ahead, providing memories that I would cherish for a lifetime. But there I sat, huddled in a small room, surrounded by a few key players, wounded, exhausted, and waiting to hear from God.

One by one the lessons came, seven in all, as my halftime unfolded.

- Lesson 1: Silence is bliss. You cannot hear from God amidst the noise of a roaring crowd. Pull back. "Be still and know that I am God," (Psalm 46:10).
- Lesson 2: It's healing time. It's a perfect time to bandage your cuts, rub out the cramps, tighten your equipment . . . well, you get the idea.
- Lesson 3: Rest for a moment. Rest is necessary for true progress. Even in war, they make time for R & R.
- Lesson 4: Surround yourself. Huddle with those that

understand your situation. Strive to keep the group small, for you cannot get consensus from the masses.

- Lesson 5: Admit your mistakes. Everyone makes mistakes. Winners turn stumbling blocks into stepping stones.
- Lesson 6: Listen to coaching. Those who have gone before you can point out the pitfalls ahead, enabling you to avoid the same traps that brought their defeat.
- Lesson 7: Play like a winner. Victory is always ahead. Forget those things that are behind you. There will be plenty of time for reflection when the game is over.

The horn is sounding; halftime has ended. Let's play ball!

You cannot hear from God
amidst the noise
of a roaring crowd.

TRUST

Luke 12 tells the story of a rich man who was the sugar daddy of his day. Assessing his financial independence, he said, "Tomorrow I will begin building bigger barns to properly care for my ever-growing surplus." Then the Lord said, "You fool, you'll be dead before the day is over—then what?" Now, typically we use this parable to minister a message of salvation and repentance. However, I want to look at it from a different angle. Let's use this as a starting point to ponder the topic of security.

This man had no doubts what tomorrow would bring. He was blessed, and day after day he expected more of the same. Little did he know that within a few hours, the world as he knew it would completely change.

The truth is, we're never as secure as we think we are.

On the heels of the Industrial Revolution, the west found itself staring in the eyes of The Great Depression. The Great Depression was a worldwide economic crisis. In the United States, it was marked by widespread unemployment and nearly ended industrial production as well as construction. The stock market plummeted 89 percent! October 29, 1929, would be known in history as Black Tuesday. It was the day the Dow Jones Industrial Average fell almost 23 percent and the market lost between $8 billion and $9 billion in value. That day had such an impact that the market did not recover from the lows of 1929 until 1954, long after WWII.

By 1932, the unemployment rate had soared past 20 percent. Thousands of banks and businesses failed. Millions were homeless. Men and women returned home from fruitless job hunts to find their dwellings padlocked. Their possessions and families were forced to a life on the streets. Many drifted from town to town looking for nonexistent jobs. Many more lived at the edges of cities in makeshift communities. People foraged in dumps and garbage cans for food. Our country's security was gone!

One author wrote, "History would suggest that once every couple of generations, there is a 'cleansing cycle' that occurs within the financial markets, society, and even within humanity as a whole. Financial institutions collapse, diseases rage, locusts fly, hailstones fall, earthquakes increase, volcanoes rumble, sunspots explode out from our heat source, wars erupt, and despotism reigns supreme."

As I write this entry, everything in my life is shifting. For the last several years, our family has been very stable and financially secure. We have never been filthy rich by the American standard, but we've been more than blessed. However, the last twelve months have been rough! Very rough! All year we've been downsizing and trimming off much of the unnecessary things that strain our finances. I currently have nine totally different resumes on file, and jobs I turned down a year ago sound really great at the moment. I've never been so unsure of tomorrow as I am today. There's a picture on our dresser that reads, "Don't be afraid of tomorrow, for God is already there."

Has life ever thrown you a curve ball?

You want to hear something ironic?

Today I was doing some consultant work for an organization that is struggling in an area. There I was, trying to help a team of people secure the future of their company while I was falling apart inside. How outrageous is that? On my way home, I started to vent. I told the Lord everything I thought about how He was doing "or not doing" His job. Then something occurred to me . . . isn't God's ultimate plan to bring me to a place where I trust Him? Totally, completely, absolutely, fully, and utterly trust Him. Isn't that what God is after? When I can say like Job, "The Lord gives and the Lord takes away. Blessed be the name of the Lord," then I know that I've got it.

As a leader, I've always been taught the importance of vision casting—knowing where I'm going and communicating it clearly to those around me. Although I agree wholeheartedly, at the same time, during this season of my life, I have no idea where I'm going. But Abraham had no idea where he was headed either. God told him to leave where he was, so Abraham started walking. Without any direction, he left the security of his surroundings and moved into uncertainty. In the middle of the unknown, he trusted God. Don't get me wrong; God's not playing games with us. Ups and downs are a part of the broken world that we live in. It rains on the just and the unjust. However, during life's highs and lows, we recognize what we put our trust in. I remember someone saying, "You can tell a lot about someone by what he reaches for on his way down." Do we really believe that He is our shepherd and because of that, we shall not be in want? Be proactive yes, but when unsure, trust Him. He knows your rising up and your lying down. Before you were formed in your mother's womb, He knew you. Only He sees the ending before the beginning.

A couple years ago, while ministering in the Cincinnati, Ohio, area, I met a trailblazer by the name of James Baldwin. He and his wife, Christina, are a living testimony of trusting God and living by faith. I dare say there are only a handful of people who reach as many youth for Jesus as James and Christina. James has proven to be a catalyst in his work with YWAM (Youth With A Mission). After hearing one of their amazing God stories, I asked them to write it down so I could share it with you. Thanks, you two!

> When I proposed to my wife, her parents gave us $1000 for a wedding dress, shoes, etc.—a great gift, but not enough for all those items, and that was all we had. That week, Christina felt the LORD told her to give the $1000 away. She called me to let me know. The same night she gave the money away, a lady approached her to congratulate her on the engagement and asked her if she had someone to make her dress because the LORD just told her to make it for us for FREE! The lady was an award-winning designer who specialized in wedding dress fashion. We ended up with a $6000 wedding dress for nothing!

Most of my favorite memories revolve around God's very great desire to "wow" me, as Mike Bickle would say. You can build your history of "wows" from today onwards. Start collecting them. Give your iPod away, do something amazing for the Kingdom, pinpoint someone on the street/at school and tell them about Jesus, buy someone's lunch.

God loves to "wow" us. Just coz He likes us. And just coz it's fun.

If you've been let down, it wasn't by God. He is your loving Daddy—and He's looking for the next chance to "wow" you. Just coz He likes you!

A PIONEER'S JOURNAL:

Feelings of security are false unless they are founded in God and His Word.

What securities are you trusting in, both false and true?

Abraham did not know where he was going. God told him to go to a country that he knew not. One preacher said it like this, "Abraham headed for the land of Know Not." In Genesis 12:1, God told Abram, "Leave your country, your relatives, your father's house, and go to a land that I will show you."

Leave, go, show. First comes the leaving, the going, then comes the showing.

What is the difference of leaving and going?

How can you translate and apply this truth to your situation?

FAMILIARITY

Sometimes it's easier to be in a familiar place of misery than in a safe place of uncertainty. In the wilderness, the children of Israel longed to return to Egyptian bondage. Even though the slavery was brutal, in Egypt they knew what to expect. Although God had proven His protection over them in the wilderness, the uncertainty of each day was more than they could bear. They had to completely depend on God for each meal, and they had no idea when they would come upon the next water hole. As a result, they preferred misery over uncertainty. We do too!

We are creatures of habit. Research says anything you do for thirty days becomes a habit. Imagine how deeply settled some of our habits are. Beside an old washed-out Alabama road, there's a sign that reads, "Choose your rut carefully, you'll be in it for the next 50 miles." Ruts are like soft beds—easy to get into, hard to get out of. Someone once said, "The second part of a man's life is made up of nothing but the habits acquired during the first half of his life."

Years ago, I read a story about a church that hired a consultant. The church was over seventy-five years old and had been on a decline for more than a decade. After spending a week previewing services and activities, the consultant met with the pastor and board and offered one suggestion. He said, "Build a fence around the property and charge visitors a $10 admission to see how church was done fifty years ago." In John Maxwell's words, "If the horse is dead—dismount." In my experience, I've come to believe that it's easier to start something than it is to redirect something. If you don't believe me, try to push a stopped car; then stand in the middle of the freeway and attempt to redirect one. Which is more challenging?

Benny Profit, the founder of First Priority, once asked me two questions:

1. How many people do you know who have given birth?
2. How many people do you know who have raised the dead?

I remember him telling me that it's easier to give birth to something new than it is to raise something old from the dead [paraphrase].

As I mentioned before, at this moment in my life I'm a very frustrated person. Can I dump my aggravation on you for a minute? For the past fourteen years, I've worked in the local church as a student pastor. During the last eight years, I've been involved in much of the pastoral activities. All I've ever known is church work. That's been my life. However, now I'm at a place where I sense God doing something different in me. Although I believe I'll return to that line of ministry, today the Lord is leading me somewhere new. At times, the uncertainty is more than I can deal with.

Earlier this year, I had a couple opportunities to return to the usual. Instead, I started applying for jobs totally outside of the norm. Dealing with the change and God's silence has been quite irritating. Every day I ask God, "What are you doing? What do you want from me?" God may not be the author of confusion, but someone sure forged His name to the story of my life because I'm clueless! But maybe that's where God wants me. Could it be that from time to time, God conceals His purposes so we can live in His promises? If you're in a similar season as I am, together let's allow God to stretch us. Why not make Romans 12:1–2 a daily prayer during this time, saying each morning, "Lord, I present my body to You as a living sacrifice, holy, and acceptable in Your sight. This is my reasonable service, and the least that I could do in light of what You have done for me. I refuse to be conformed to this world, but I will be transformed by the renewing of my mind. Through this time in my life, You will prove to me and through me

what is Your good and acceptable and perfect will. Thank You for
Your strength, oh Lord."

Sandra Saylor has been helping me co-author books for the
past couple years. Sandra's the one who brings you the reflection
questions at the end of each chapter. Sandra concludes this chapter
with the following words of encouragement:

"I love Jason's tag line, *Simplifying the Search for God's Will.* I
can actually hear our readers sigh with relief! When I came to the
realization that God is not trying to hide His will from me in some
divine guessing game and that He will actually make it hard for me
to miss His will, I experienced such an alleviation of anxiety.

"According to Romans 12:1–2, my greatest responsibility is
to give myself to God, and that involves the giving of my own will
to Him: my dreams and aspirations, my mistakes and failures, my
accomplishments and achievements. It came down to a *simple* trust
issue. Do I truly trust Him with my life and my future?

"Secondly, this verse tells me that I am to allow God to
transform my thinking. My thinking is transformed by using His
Word to police my thoughts. It is unmistakable, unequivocal,
absolute, and indisputable that His will for you and for me is to
know His Word. As I become conformed to His Word, so does
my thinking.

"I know there are times when things are extremely
complicated and this Scripture passage simply does not seem to
suffice. However, as we give our will to Him and give our mind
to His Word, He will make sure we are walking smack dab in the
middle of His will!"

A PIONEER'S JOURNAL:

Even though God provided manna for the children
of Israel while they were in the wilderness, it wasn't what they
wanted. What God had designed to build their faith, turned into a
four thousand-year lesson on how *not* to act while in a wilderness
experience!

What manna are you complaining about?

RED LIGHT–GREEN LIGHT

Do you remember playing Red Light–Green Light when you were a kid? The idea was simple. Choose one player to be Red Light. He stands a few yards from the other players, with his back turned to them. The other players line up shoulder to shoulder behind him. Their goal is to get close enough to tap Red Light on the shoulder, but they can move only when he says, "Green Light." To begin playing, Red Light closes his eyes and yells, "Green Light!" Players then run at top speed toward him until he yells, "Red Light!" and turns around as fast as he can. The instant the other players hear "Red Light!" they must stop running. Anyone Red Light sees still moving when he turns around must return to the starting line. Man, I loved that game!

Oh how I wished the Lord led us in that same kind of way. Knowing what to stop and knowing what to start are two things I've been giving much thought to. I want to be the kind of leader who knows when to start something and, just as importantly, knows when to stop something. The *stops* of a good man are ordered of the Lord as well as his *steps*. I remember hearing a preacher say, "Sometimes being in the wrong place is the result of being in the right place too long."

In Numbers 21, Israel was being devoured by fiery serpents. God told Moses to make a bronze serpent, put it on a pole, and hold it up in the air. Whoever looked upon the serpent would live. But generations later, God was angry because Israel was still carrying around the image (2 Kings 18). The manna of heaven was only good for the day in which it was given.

Some folks have a difficult time getting started. God births a dream in their heart and they just struggle with the launching process. I once heard a message titled, "Four Bones." The minister said that people basically fall into one of four categories:

1. Some are jaw bones—always talking about what they are going to do. Henry Ford said, "You can't build a reputation based upon what you say that you are going to do."
2. Some people are wish bones—hoping that someday their dreams will come true. They're just waiting, praying, believing, and wishing.
3. Others are like tail bones—these folks aren't doing anything to make their dreams a reality. An old proverb says, "God created us equal, in that He gave us two ends, one to sit with and the other to think with. Success in life depends upon which end you use the most."
4. A few are back bones—willing to do whatever it takes to see their dreams come to fruition.

Then there are those of us who have just as much trouble stopping. So often, what begins as Spirit-led ministry becomes a movement, then a monument, and ultimately a museum of what God *was doing*. Someone once asked a friend of mine to elaborate on the will of God. My friend said, "I simply keep doing whatever God told me to do last, and when He tells me to stop, I stop. It's that easy." That sounds good in theory, but it can be hard living out. Forgive me for being so cynical; it's just that so much of what we do seems to be copy-cat Christianity. It worked over there; let's do it over here. It was great then; let's do it now. Do you remember the story of Jesus healing a blind man by spitting in the dirt, making some mud, and rubbing it in his eyes? I want to know how many times the disciples tried that and got beat up for doing so. You know it happened! We get stuck in yesterday's victories, and we try to duplicate it everywhere we go.

In the book of Acts, the Lord worked strange miracles through the apostles. In one account, pieces of their dirty, sweat-stained garments were taken to the sick and oppressed and they were healed. Today you can buy nice, perfectly shaped, little white scissor-cut prayer cloths with cute zigzag edges to distribute to those in need of prayer. For a few extra bucks, you can market your miracle by getting your ministry's name and Web address printed on one side. Doesn't that turn your stomach? Doesn't it seem as though something's missing—that perhaps somewhere, at some point, God moved on, and we're stuck in the rut? Of course, there are many foundational things we can never stray from. Everything else is up for trial.

A PIONEER'S JOURNAL:

Long-time pastor, mentor, and church planter, Charles Simpson, said, "The message never changes but the methods do."
What is the message that never changes?

What are some methods that have changed through the years?

FROM ONE TRAILBLAZER TO ANOTHER
Finding the Will of God by D. P. Franks

The small parsonage and white church in Southern Illinois had the appearance of a picture right out of a magazine. The surrounding fields and farms provided small game hunting unrivaled anywhere! The rural area was perfect for me. Having worked in Ohio and feeling very out of place in the city, we had returned to my hometown in Southwest Virginia two years earlier. It was home, and I had a job I loved. There was, however, a call in my heart that was not being fulfilled. When the church at Dale contacted my young wife and me, it was as if heaven had spoken. There was no debate, very little discussion, and no regret. We put everything we had in a U-Haul truck and left our newly purchased home for our first "God Assignment." From the day we took our wedding vows, we had been committed to doing the "will of God" above everything else. When the call came, it was as if the decision had been made years earlier and it never occurred to us to say, "No!" That commitment had its rewards! Tracing their existence as a congregation to the Azusa Street Revival in Los Angeles, California, these farmers knew how to make church exciting. They believed in a Living Lord and were bold in their testimonies as to His power to change lives! They were real, earthy, honest, hardworking people with real faith. It was an honor to be their pastor.

Knowing our tenure was coming to a close, restlessness began to invade our thinking and ministry. It was time to leave.

Where would we go? What would we do? Calls came from other congregations, but uncertainty rose in our hearts as to the will of God. As the frustration grew in my own spirit, I sought counsel from my pastor who happened to also be my father-in-law. He listened patiently for several weeks to my confused ramblings and questions. If he tried to advise me during that time, I suppose his voice could not be heard over the mumbling and groaning of my own confused and frustrated spirit. When I finally allowed him to speak he asked, "Do you remember how you felt when you knew it was time to come here?" "I certainly do," I responded. "That is exactly how you will feel when it comes time to leave," he said. Instantly, a calm came over me, and all the wrestling of my soul ceased. He was telling me the truth, and I recognized it! I had not been able to hear God because of the turmoil I had created in my own heart. My wife and I made a decision that day not to be anxious about where to go or what to do. When the Lord was ready, He would make His will known, and until then all our fretting was worse than useless; it was destructive and debilitating.

In the months that followed, we saw more people come to a saving knowledge of Christ than over the entire period of time we had served that congregation. The apostle Paul wrote to the Colossian Church about doing the will of God. In the midst of great practical instructions about "whatever you do . . ." (Colossians 3:17, 23), he offered two words of enormous spiritual uplift. ". . . [L]et the peace of God rule . . . let the word of Christ dwell . . ." (Colossians 3:15–16). Those are the only two things a believer needs in order to find and follow the will of God. Fill your mind and spirit with His illuminating Word, and He will give you His Peace concerning the path you are to travel.

Do you remember how you felt
when you knew it was time to come here?
That is exactly how you will feel
when it comes time to leave.

MOSAIC LIVING

It's the day after Thanksgiving. Most hardworking men would be at home watching football or *Rambo* or something, but not me. Since Melissa is working and my thirteen-year-old daughter has a whopping $150, I was nominated to drive 110 miles to experience the worst shopping day of the year with my wonderful little girl. After that experience, I'm pretty sure I could write one of those *Six Hours in Hell* books. Perhaps the coolest thing I saw today was a 20" x 14" mosaic of Van Gogh's *Starry Night*—and it was on sale for $800! I was an art major in college, and although Melissa respects my love for interesting art, I doubt she would have given me wall space for the well-priced-one-of-a-kind piece. Mosaics have always fascinated me. In case you weren't an art major, a mosaic is a piece of artwork comprised of a multitude of tiny pieces (in this case, used press-on nails—how tasteful). Although each piece seems meaningless by itself, in relationship with the others, it adds to the image's clarity. In many ways, discovering God's will functions much like a beautiful mosaic.

For years I've made the habit of journaling thoughts—not just the superspiritual ones, but the where-did-that-come-from thoughts as well. I've jotted things on the back of business cards, napkins, shopping lists, phone bills—even toilet paper! Yes, God can speak to you in there, too. Some call it, "Going boldly before the throne."

Over the years, I've filed my scribbles into a variety of categories. Time and time again, I've witnessed one random thought snowball into countless confirmations. It's kind of like buying a car that no one else has, then passing a thousand just like it on the way home—once you got it, you saw it everywhere. When God wants to speak to you, He'll go to any and every extreme to get your attention.

But He's subtle.

He threw Himself on a bush to get Moses' attention, but it wasn't a nearby bush. It was close enough to be seen, but just far enough to be out of the way. When Jesus came walking across the water, the Bible says that He would have passed them by had the disciples not cried out. Overlooking Jerusalem, Jesus wept because the Kingdom of Heaven had appeared, but they missed the day of their visitation. The good news is God wants to be heard. Through an endless number of ways, He'll plaster His thoughts everywhere we go. Just a few hours ago, I was having dinner with my two kids. Melissa and I've been talking a good deal about relocating. Tori's in middle school, so the thought of a new school is a challenge for her. Over dinner, Tori asked, "Where do you think we're going to move to, and when?" I told her the Lord had always led our family in the past and He would continue to lead us now. He knows what's best and He will lead us to the right place. He will keep leading and we must keep moving as He leads. After paying for our meal, we hopped in the truck, turned on the radio, and the 80s song, "Funky Town," was playing. The first verse said, "Got to make a move to a town that is right for me." Tori started laughing. I started laughing. I'm sure God was laughing too. We've been talking and praying seriously about starting a new church. I went to a movie two nights after our "Funky Town" laugh, and as I leaned back in my comfy theater chair, the first commercial began. Here's what the commercial said: "Start a new church here today! Visit us online to find out how." Then a Web site appeared and the next commercial began. I was going crazy. And the spokesperson for the ad sounded like God too. Isn't that crazy? Does God know how to speak to us or what?

As a kid, I used to love hidden picture puzzles. The children's magazines in the lobby of my dentist's office had tons of them. The enjoyment of those games made the pain of cavity filling worthwhile. Each hidden object was camouflaged just enough to blend in, but not so hard that you couldn't find it. That's so like God. The entire Old Testament was a giant picture puzzle—a mosaic of images, prophecies, dreams, and visions pointing toward God's plan for redemption. We see Jesus in every book from Genesis to Malachi. Throughout the book of Acts, the apostles used these Old Testament images to prove that Jesus was the Christ.

Some time back, my first cousin was at a crossroads in his career. An opportunity surfaced for him to start a business with a friend of his. At the same time, he was interviewing with several other companies within his current line of work. Facing a variety of opportunities, he began to ask God for guidance. As much as he wanted to do what most pleased God, his frustration grew over not knowing which direction to go. Then one day, while cleaning out an old work truck at his dad's farm, he found a laminated card. Written on the card were the following words:

> I believe I'm always divinely guided,
> I believe I will always be led to take the right turn in the road,
> I believe God will always make a way where there is no way.

Somewhere, there's a lament card with your name on it, and at just the right time, He'll make sure you find it . . . if it doesn't find you first.

A PIONEER'S JOURNAL:

Corrie ten Boom said in an interview before she died, "Life is like a beautiful tapestry handmade by God. We, however, only see the ugly side, the side with all the loose ends. Someday, we'll see the beauty of our lives from God's perspective."

What is success from God's perspective?

What did success look like in Jesus' life?

DREAMS

My friend, David, was having a wild dream when he woke up his wife, Stacey. To this day, David can't remember the dream, but Stacey sure remembers waking up. When she opened her eyes, he was sitting straight up in the bed, one arm fully extended, and a finger pointing toward the foot of the bed. Shouting to the top of his voice, he declared, "Behold, the pale horse! He that rides upon it is Death and Hell!" As you can imagine, Stacey nearly had a heart attack.

I remember having a reccurring dream as a child: aliens had broken into our home. I snuck through the house and into the kitchen. When I peeked over the bar counter, three of them had my mom in the laundry room. Two held her still while the third one put a spoon to her mouth. In the bowl of the spoon was a small ball of fire. Somehow that ball of fire turned humans into aliens. They made my mom eat it. Her eyes opened wide, and a freaky grin came across her face. My sweet little mommy was gone. For the next few months, I wondered. Every time she grinned, I cried and peed in my pants.

We all have dreams. Some dreams are like my weird far-out-there dream. Other dreams are manifestations of deep fears we've yet to overcome—not that I was ever afraid my mom was an alien. God also speaks to us through dreams. We see this repeatedly throughout the Bible:

Abraham's dream—Genesis 15
Abimelech's dream—Genesis 20
Jacob's dreams—Genesis 28, Genesis 31, and Genesis 46
Laban's dream—Genesis 31
Joseph's dream—Genesis 37
The cupbearer's and baker's dreams—Genesis 40
Pharaoh's dream—Genesis 41
Midianite soldier's dream—Judges 7
Solomon's dream—1 Kings 3
Nebuchadnezzar's dream—Daniel 2
Daniel's dream—Daniel 7
Joseph's dreams concerning Mary and her child—Matthew 1, 2
The dream given to the wise men—Matthew 2
Pilate's wife has a dream—Matthew 27
Paul's dream—Acts 16

In Numbers 12:6, God said, "When there is a prophet among you, I, the LORD, reveal Myself to them in visions, I speak to them in dreams . . ." One night I dreamed that someone handed me a newspaper. The front page article was about a new abstinence program that our organization was doing across the country. During this same period of time, I had been teaching on Queen Esther. Most people don't realize that only beautiful young virgins were selected to run in the queenish pageant. With that in mind, I had been teaching in our services the importance of fighting for your purity. Esther would not have been chosen to be queen had she given herself away before marriage. If Esther had not been queen, the Jews would have died. If the Jews would have died, Jesus would not have come. If Jesus would not have come, we would all be lost without hope. So I sat down with a couple of our staff and shared with them my dream and the burning desire I had to share Esther's story with young people all over the country. Someone said, "Well, what if we partner with formal-wear stores, Avon, Mary Kay, and hair salons, and do free prom makeovers on five or six girls in each school that hosts one of our events?" A lady serving on our team sent out an e-mail and within a couple of weeks, we had over $30,000 in brand-new prom dresses donated to our ministry. Several months later, the program was the headline article of an Alabama newspaper. Thank God for dreams!

I'm sure most of us know the story of Solomon and his request for wisdom, but did you know that the dialog between him and God took place during a dream? You can read it in the third chapter of 1 Kings. Dreams are more serious than we give them credit for. One of the primary ways the Lord speaks to me is through dreams. For that reason, I keep of diary of the things He's shown me during the night. One night, while I was dreaming, I woke Melissa. She said that I was speaking to a demon, demanding it to leave. For close to seven years, I had dreams like that. Every night was nonstop spiritual warfare. On that particular night, Melissa got a little freaked out, so she left the room to check on the kids. She quietly prayed over both of our children and went to the living room. For about half an hour, she sat on the coach speaking blessings over our family, and then she came back to bed. I was still sound asleep. Melissa said that when she lay down, I said, "Everything my wife has said, let it be so—amen!" If I shared all the bizarre things that I've encountered through the night, most folks would think I was the biggest liar on the planet.

Sometimes I wonder if the devil torments us with nightmares during our childhood to shut down our desire for dreaming. Begin to offer your sleep to the Lord. Each night, welcome the Holy Spirit into your time of rest. Invite Him to speak to you while you dream. As you begin dreaming, journal each morning the things you've experienced during the night. Keep in mind that not all things are obvious and clear when we dream. Throughout the Bible, many of the dreams needed an interpretation.

A few weeks ago, a friend of mine told me that she was repeatedly dreaming of digging a well in Africa. As the water gushed out of the ground, people gathered around and began to dance. Now let's think about her dream for a moment. On one hand, perhaps the Holy Spirit is telling her and her family to go dig a well in Africa, or to begin supporting a ministry that does. The first thought that came to my mind was what Africa is known for—oppression, neglect, an abused people who've been taken advantage of. Wells always represent life. Jesus offered the woman at the well Living Water that would permeate every part of her being. Could it be that the Holy Spirit was saying to my friend that in the areas where she's been abused, neglected, and mistreated, He is going to enable her to dig a well of fresh life for those who've suffered as she has? Once that well is tapped, a multitude of people will rejoice over the freedom and newness that God has brought to them through her victory. Whatever the case is, dreams are often layered; meaning you have to dig a little deeper than the obvious.

Job 33:14–16 says, "For God does speak—now one way, now another—though no one perceives it. In a dream, in a vision of the night, when deep sleep falls on people as they slumber in their beds . . ."

A PIONEER'S JOURNAL:

In Daniel 2, a most ungodly king received the most comprehensive dream concerning the governments of this world. But there was a catch . . . it took a man of God to interpret the dream. Daniel said to the king, "And it is not because I am wiser than anyone else that I know the secret of your dream, but because God wants you to understand what was in your heart" (Daniel 2:30, New Living Translation).

God wants the world to know what they're dreaming about. He wants them to understand His messages to them in the night.

Do you see ungodly people as prospective containers of God-given, revelatory dreams?

Why do you think God didn't give the dream to Daniel first?

Dreams, many times, are like parables—full of hidden meaning (Reference Matthew 13:10–13).

How is a person's curiosity and interest linked to their ability to find understanding?

WHO'S GOT YOUR EAR?

There's an old saying that goes like this: "When I was eighteen, my father was so ignorant I could hardly stand to have the old man around. When I was twenty-five, I was amazed at how much he had learned in seven years." I will admit, there were times I doubted the wisdom of my father, but after Melissa and I were married, had two kids, a few pets, and a bunch of bills, I took his advice more seriously. Now, every day I get older, he get sharper. There's no reward for resisting the guidance of those who've gone before you. Looking back, I realize that those who listen the least, do the least in life.

A great example of this is found in the story of Solomon's son and successor, Rehoboam. Under his reign, the magnificent kingdom took a plunge from its pinnacle of glory. Ten of the twelve tribes of Israel broke away from his kingdom and formed their own country. Rehoboam ruled the southern kingdom, known as Judah. In the midst of the chaos, Jerusalem was devastated by Shishak, king of Egypt (2 Chronicles 12:2–9). And what led to his demise was his choice of advisors. The northern tribes were tired of breaking their backs on the king's pet building projects and paying for them with high taxes. So they asked Solomon's son, the new king, to ease up on them and lighten their load. Rehoboam consulted with his father's advisors and they gave him wise counsel. They advised him to lighten their load, and by doing so he would gain their loyalty. But the young king would not give ear to their instruction. We find the story in 2 Chronicles chapter 10.

2 Chronicles 10:1–14

And Rehoboam went to Shechem, for all Israel had gone to Shechem to make him king. So it happened, when Jeroboam the son of Nebat heard it (he was in Egypt, where he had fled from the presence of King Solomon), that Jeroboam returned from Egypt. Then they sent for him and called him. And Jeroboam and all Israel came and spoke to Rehoboam, saying, "Your father made our yoke heavy; now therefore, lighten the burdensome service of your father and his heavy yoke which he put on us, and we will serve you."

So he said to them, "Come back to me after three days." And the people departed.

Then King Rehoboam consulted the elders who stood before his father Solomon while he still lived, saying, "How do you advise me to answer these people?" And they spoke to him, saying, "If you are kind to these people, and please them, and speak good words to them, they will be your servants forever." But he rejected the advice which the elders had given him, and consulted the young men who had grown up with him, who stood before him. And he said to them, "What advice do you give? How should we answer this people who have spoken to me, saying, 'Lighten the yoke which your father put on us'?" Then the young men who had grown up with him spoke to him, saying, "Thus you should speak to the people who have spoken to you, saying, 'Your father made our yoke heavy, but you make it lighter on us'—thus you shall say to them: 'My little finger shall be thicker than my father's waist! And now, whereas my father put a heavy yoke on you, I will add to your yoke; my father chastised you with whips, but I will chastise you with scourges!'" So Jeroboam and all the people came to Rehoboam on the third day, as the king had directed, saying, "Come back to me the third day."

Then the king answered them roughly. King Rehoboam rejected the advice of the elders, and he spoke to them according to the advice of the young men, saying, "My father made your yoke heavy, but I will add to it; my father chastised you with whips, but I will chastise you with scourges!"

Allowing the wrong people to speak into his life caused the foolish king more than he expected. Not only did Rehoboam fail to receive taxes from the ten northern tribes, but his kingdom had to pay tribute to the Egyptian Pharaoh.

If you want to know where you'll be two years from now, just look at the people around you. Our friends are like a prophecy of our future direction and character. For this reason, Proverbs 12:26 says, "The righteous should choose his friends carefully, for the way of the wicked leads them astray." Anyone can tell you what you want to hear, but a true friend will tell you what you need to hear. You see, we all have blind spots, areas in our lives that we fail to see. That's why we need people around us who can diagnose our places of need. Proverbs 12:15 says, "The way of a fool is right in his own eyes, but he who heeds counsel is wise." There have been times in my life when I've felt so sure about a direction, only to have someone close to me question the decision. Looking back, I realize those folks helped me avoid some serious mistakes. I'm not suggesting we give ear to everyone. You know what you get when you ask 100 people for advice? You get 100 different opinions. However, all of us need a few people around us that speak into our lives. One of my favorite Proverbs is verse five of chapter twenty. It says that purpose in the heart of a man is like a deep well of water, but a man of understanding knows how to draw it out. Be sure of this: when God has a plan for you, He will always put someone in your life to help. When Satan has a plan for you, he will always put someone in your life to help as well.

It kind of reminds me of a story I heard years ago. One winter's day, a farmer was driving to town when he noticed a wounded bird lying on the side of the road. He desperately wanted to help the poor bird, but he was already running late for a lunch meeting with a potential business partner. Then the farmer noticed a warm, steamy pile of poop near the cold, wounded bird. The caring farmer brought his pickup to a stop, picked the bird up, and plopped it in the poop, leaving only its head to show. He gently said to the bird, "This spot will keep you warm until I return. Then I'll take you home with me until you're all better." As the truck drove away, the warm bird began to chirp and sing away. It was at that moment that a hawk heard the trapped bird, swooped down, and ate the bird with one giant GUMP! What's the moral of the story? The one that put you in the poop is not necessarily your enemy, and the one who gets you out of the poop is not necessarily your friend. Rehoboam was swallowed up by the trouble caused by his "so-called friends."

Sadly, for many of us, we choose to only give ear to the "big shots," the guys at the top, those who sell the most books, dazzle the largest crowds, and lead the greatest empires. It's an unfortunate mistake to ignore the wisdom of seasoned men and women of God because they're unknown by the masses. Success is not being the greatest; rather it's being who God called you to be. The greatest coaches are certainly not the greatest players. Behind every great man of God is an unfamiliar saint, unheard of by the world. Treasure those the Lord has put in your life to guide you through your journey. On down the road you'll be glad you listened.

A PIONEER'S JOURNAL:

Why are blind spots called blind spots?

Does everyone have blind spots?

What creates blind spots?

What are the consequences of blind spots?

Who in your life have you given the permission to point out your blind spots?

What are some important qualities and characteristics of someone you would choose to fill that role in your life?

JOY FOR THE JOURNEY

When what used to bring me joy now leaves me drained and burdened, I have to ask myself, "What's God trying to say?" Doing God's will requires our participation, but in the middle of our labor, God always gives joy for the journey. The disciples had the stew beat out of them, but even during those times, they celebrated with unexplainable joy. Over and over, God's Word promises us peace and joy. He said, "I will go with you and give you rest." So, if there's an absence of peace and joy, what am I to assume? Is God still with me? Sure, He lives in me, but is He still involved in my activities? During times like this, I ask myself two questions:

1. How's my relationship with Jesus? Am I still spending time in His Presence? Do I still spend time getting lost in His Word? It's His Spirit and Word that fills me with the fresh passion I need to do what I do. We must withdraw from the work and allow Him to refill what we've given away. Like Granny used to say, "It's hard for an empty sack to stand up." I've learned that if the devil can't make you bad, he'll make you busy!

2. Do I need to keep doing this? Has God moved on? Is He leading me somewhere new? Have I become so busy that I've missed something along the way?

Perhaps the reason we feel burnt out and stretched to the max is because we're doing things He's no longer a part of. A pastor once asked, "If the Holy Spirit left the church, how much of its activities would continue on unfazed by His absence?" Jesus never ran late for meetings, He was never out of breath or red faced; yet He accomplished more in three years' time than the church has in two thousand years. But you're thinking, "Yeah, and He was the Son of God!" Yes, but didn't He say, "Great things will you do because I go to My Father"? You see, Jesus chased after the Father; everything else chased after Him. He only did what He saw the Father do, and you and I have to get to that same place.

At times, I feel like the guys who had fished all night but caught nothing; all my labor is wasted away on fruitless activities. Once those guys encountered Jesus, they knew right where to go and exactly what they needed to do. In only a few minutes, they saw more results than in an entire night of labor. Now who doesn't want more return for less work? You know the old cliché, "Work smarter, not harder." One guy said to his employer, "I've been here eleven years doing three men's work for one man's pay. Now I want a raise." His boss said, "Well, I can't give you a raise, but if you'll tell me who the other two men are, I'll fire them."

We often confuse motion and progress. The more we're doing, the more progress we're making. But a rocking horse keeps moving without making any progress. God's called us to be fruitful, not busy. If anyone had the opportunity to always be "on the go," Jesus did; however, He seemed to have no problem resisting opportunities that the Father did not endorse. Like someone once told me, "If you can't say no to men, you'll never be able to say yes to God." So where's your joy level today? If it's low, why? Take a moment and allow the Holy Spirit to begin speaking to you concerning His involvement in your current activities.

A PIONEER'S JOURNAL:

The joy from reading and understanding the Word of God produces a refuge, a stronghold, and a place of safety.

How much time do you regularly spend reading and meditating on the Word of God?

Do you understand what you are reading?

With whom do you discuss Scripture and its meaning?

What kind of joy is produced when you receive a "rhema" (a clear word, an idea) from God's Word?

MY SHEEP KNOW MY VOICE

When a zebra is born, its mother circles it over and over. She presses closely against her colt's frail body and moves around and around. For days, she does this. Why? She wants her colt to memorize her stripes. You see, each zebra has a unique stripe pattern. Their stripes are like our fingerprints; no two zebras have the same. By memorizing its mother's stripes, the colt can quickly identify its mother among a herd of others.

Jesus said, "Most assuredly, I say to you, he who does not enter the sheepfold by the door, but climbs up some other way, the same is a thief and a robber. But he who enters by the door is the shepherd of the sheep. To him the doorkeeper opens, and the sheep hear his voice; and he calls his own sheep by name and leads them out. And when he brings out his own sheep, he goes before them; and the sheep follow him, for they know his voice. Yet they will by no means follow a stranger, but will flee from him, for they do not know the voice of strangers" (John 10:1–5).

Several years ago, I was speaking in a church on the subject of knowing God's voice. I began by saying to the congregation, "I'm going to ask you a series of questions. After each question, I want you to shout the answer back to me." The questions were:

1. Ladies, what's your favorite chick flick?
2. Guys, what's your favorite action movie?
3. Kids, what's your favorite horror film?
4. Everyone, what's your favorite TV show?

5. Moms and Dads, what's your favorite 80s song?
6. Everyone, what's your favorite Bible verse?

With no hesitation, folks screamed out their answers to the first five questions. But when I asked the final question, there was an uncomfortable moment of silence. It was like the energy level completely left the building. A few dozen people fumbled for an answer, but even then the answers were muffled. My dear friend, if you wish to discover the voice of God, learn the Word of God. Those who know God's Word the best, hear God's voice the most. Jesus said, "Man shall not live by bread alone, but by every word that proceeds from the mouth of God" (Matthew 4:4). God's voice will never contradict His Word.

Psalm 19:7–14
The law of the Lord is perfect, converting the soul; the testimony of the Lord is sure, making wise the simple; the statutes of the Lord are right, rejoicing the heart; the commandment of the Lord is pure, enlightening the eyes; the fear of the Lord is clean, enduring forever; the judgments of the Lord are true and righteous altogether. More to be desired are they than gold, Yea, than much fine gold; sweeter also than honey and the honey comb. Moreover by them Your servant is warned, and in keeping them there is great reward. Who can understand his errors? Cleanse me from secret faults. Keep back Your servant also from presumptuous sins; let them not have dominion over me. Then I shall be blameless, and I shall be innocent of great transgression. Let the words of my mouth and the meditation of my heart be acceptable in Your sight, O Lord, my strength and my Redeemer.

Notice the words and phrases associated with God's Word in that passage:

- perfect
- sure

- right
- rejoicing
- pure
- enlightening
- clean
- enduring forever
- true and righteous altogether
- better than fine gold
- sweeter than honey
- rewarding

Several weeks ago, I was eating dinner with a young man who happens to be a Muslim. I'm always eager to learn why people believe what they believe so I began asking him some questions concerning his faith. For starters, I asked what a typical service was like at the mosque. My friend said, "We don't gather for what you call a service; when we gather it's for the purpose of corporate prayer." Wanting to know more I asked, "Yeah, but what about the music and teaching? How does that part of your time together look?" With a big grin he looked down and, shaking his head, he said, "We're not like you guys. You all say the Bible is the most important book on the planet, but you pay some other guy to learn what it says and teach it to you and your children. You know who taught me the Koran? My parents. You know who taught my parents the Koran? Their parents. You want to guess who will teach my children the Koran? My wife and I. No big shot communicator is getting rich off teaching us our book. We love it, we learn it, and we pass it on to the next generation."

I was speechless.

And terribly convicted for my failure.

My friend had rightly pinned us well.

How can I say the Bible is the inspired Word of God and not feast from its pages every single day? Why would I not put it to memory? How could I let days and weeks pass without sharing its promises with my children? How can I expect God's guidance in my life when I don't even take the time to study what He's already said?

Nothing is more important than the Word of God. Have you ever been in a crowded area and thought you heard the voice of someone you know? Above all the other voices you heard a familiar sound. The more acquainted you are with someone's voice, the easier it is to distinguish it above all the others. So it is with God's voice. Each time you read His Word, you hear the sound of His voice. It's His Word that becomes a lamp to your feet and a light to your path (Psalm 119:105).

A PIONEER'S JOURNAL:

Psalm 103:7 says, "He made known his ways unto Moses, his acts unto the children of Israel." The masses can see God's acts, but fewer will know God's ways.

What do you think is required to "know God's ways?"

Reference Moses' life. How did Moses learn the ways of God?

FROM ONE TRAILBLAZER TO ANOTHER
Ears to Hear by Brad Freeman

"Do you know why you don't hear me?"

"No, Lord," I answered.
"Because you're not listening."

Does God speak today? Acts 2:17–19 says the outpouring of God's Spirit is marked by dreams, visions, prophecy, signs, and wonders. I believe this describes an explosion of divine communication available to everyone.

God still speaks. John 1:1 says He is the Word. He is not the silence. God speaks through dreams, visions, prophecy, an audible voice, a still small voice, an inward witness, signs, circumstances, people, angels, animals, nature, supernatural works, and many other ways.

The real question is not, "Does God speak?" The real question is, "Am I listening?" I love to listen when I have a big decision to make. But am I willing to listen in the check-out line at Wal-Mart when He wants me to tell the check-out girl that He still loves her and wants her back!

We must have ears to hear. The Jews rejected Jesus and stoned Stephen because, as Stephen said, their hearts and ears were uncircumcised. As we cleanse ourselves of selfish motives and desires and deepen our relationship with God through prayer, study, fellowship, and sharing life adventures with Him, we will grow in our ability to hear and discern His voice. Even the great prophet,

Samuel, had to learn how to recognize the audible voice of God.

Hearing God is not about finding the right formula either. Folks often say things like, "If God speaks to me, I'll know it!" or "If God opens the door, it must be time to leave." Well, God spoke to Samuel with an audible voice and to the Jews God spoke through Jesus, and in both examples, they failed to recognize what they had heard as the voice of God. God opened prison doors for Paul and Silas in Acts 16, and they had the sensitivity to know that even though God opened the door, it wasn't time to leave.

There are other voices speaking too—people, demons, circumstances, our own minds. In Matthew 16, Satan spoke through one in Jesus' inner circle—Peter.

Even though we face a lot of challenges to hearing God, the rewards are awesome! We will see God do incredible things in and through us. We can all develop ears to hear by offering ourselves to the Holy Spirit, developing a mindset based on Scripture, and a heartset of love.

The real question is not,

Does God speak?

The real question is,

Am I listening?

Even the great prophet, Samuel, had to learn how to recognize the audible voice of God.

NOTHING BUT TROUBLE

For most of my Christian life, I longed to be in God's will. In my mind, living out His wishes would be like a Jedi's harmony with The Force. By aligning myself with God's plan, incredible power would be released in me and through me. With this power, I could ward off any unwanted dangers, conquer every problem, and if need be, lift my X-Wing Fighter from the swamps of Dagobah.

Did I mention I was a *Star Wars* fan?

But what if God's will doesn't involve getting you out of trouble? Better yet, what if God's will involves putting you right in the middle of trouble? To think anything different, you would have to overlook the majority of people in Scripture who lived in His will. John the Baptist lost his head while living in God's will. Jesus was beaten, mocked, and crucified in accordance to God's will. Consider Paul's testimony concerning the things he faced while doing God's will. He told the believers in Corinth that he was:

- Beaten and striped above measure
- Frequently imprisoned
- Often faced death
- Nearly killed on five different occasions after being beaten by the Jews
- Three times beaten with rods
- Once stoned
- Three times shipwrecked
- Spent a night and a day floating in the deep sea

- Constantly on the move
- In deadly waters
- Surrounded by robbers
- Left naked
- Freezing to death
- Threatened by his own countrymen
- Threatened by the Gentiles
- In danger in the city
- In danger in the wilderness
- In danger at sea
- Set up by false brethren
- Weary often
- Weak and exhausted
- Without sleep
- Near starvation
- Dehydrated
- Committed to fasting
- And he said that these were the conditions he lived in "daily."
  2 Corinthians 11:23–28

Anyone desiring to follow Jesus understood that trouble came with the package. Jesus told an eager new recruit, "Foxes have holes, birds have nests, but I don't have any place to lay my head." That was His way of saying, "This won't always be easy." Following Jesus meant that you signed up for better or worse. We don't know much about this kind of commitment in our American world. We live in the land of love 'em and leave 'em. Take care of number one. Fight for what's best for you. But Jesus wasn't like us. So the question is, "How much like Jesus do we want to be?" 1 Peter 2:21 says, "For to this you were called, because Christ also suffered for us, leaving us an example, that you should follow His steps." Did you get that? We were called to suffering. Jesus welcomed anyone who desired to accompany Him by saying, "Take up your cross and follow Me."

There was once a man who felt as though he could carry his troubles no further. One night while he slept, he dreamed he carried his cross into heaven. Laying his burden before the Lord, he said, "Master, this load is far too heavy for me to carry." Jesus said, "I understand, My child. However, everyone has a cross to bear. But if you wish, you can trade your cross for another." With a sigh of relief, the man happily agreed. Jesus took the man's cross and disappeared behind a giant door. A few minutes later, the Lord returned. Standing beside the open door, Jesus said, "In this warehouse, you'll find a variety of crosses, burdens of many shapes and sizes. Choose any cross you wish, My son."

The man could hardly believe his eyes. There seemed to be no end to the height or length of the warehouse. And the crosses—they were huge! Carefully he searched for his new cross. His search continued for what seemed like days. Then in the corner, he spotted the perfect load—a tiny cross that paled in comparison to the heavy burdens surrounding it. Picking it up, he ran to the Lord and said, "This is the one! I'll carry this one, Lord!" Jesus said, "Well, my child, this is the cross you brought to Me."

A PIONEER'S JOURNAL:

What's the moral of the story? Your neighbor's troubles are never as bad as yours, but their kids are always worse.

So back to the question, "What if God's will involves putting you right in the middle of trouble? What then? Do you stay committed? Do you stick it out? If so, why? What's there to look forward to?"

Remember, troubled seas make good sailors and great captains. Like a buddy of mine once said, "You can only have power over the storms you can sleep through."

THE PART PRAYER PLAYS

Nothing lies beyond the reach of prayer, except that which lies outside of the will of God. It's impossible to live a healthy Christian life apart from prayer, but through an intimate relationship with Christ, all things become possible. A prayer-filled life is a power-filled life. On the flip side, seven days without prayer makes one weak. The history of the church's progress is the history of prayer.

> Elijah prayed and called down fire from heaven.
> Daniel prayed and was saved from the hungry lions.
> One hundred twenty people prayed and the church was born.
> Paul prayed and the prison walls were shaken.
> Luther prayed and the gates of Rome shook.
> Knox prayed and Queen Mary trembled.
> Wesley prayed and a great revival swept through England.
> Müller prayed and orphanages sprang up.
> Roberts prayed and the Holy Spirit was poured out in Wales.

The question is, "What is being shaped because of your prayers?"

Silence and solitude were regular disciplines in Jesus' life. The evening before He chose His disciples, Jesus spent the entire night in prayer (Luke 6). In Mark 1:35, we see Jesus rising long before daylight, and finding a solitary place to pray. After feeding the 5,000, Jesus sent the multitudes away (Mark 6). The disciples boarded a boat and pushed off toward the other side. But Jesus departed to the mountain to pray. While He prayed, a storm swept across the Sea of Galilee, threatening the life of His disciples. However, Jesus continued in prayer until the fourth watch of the night; then He came walking on the water. The fourth watch was the hours of 3:00–6:00 a.m. Luke 5:16 says, "He Himself often withdrew into the wilderness and prayed." Luke wrote, "And in the daytime He was teaching in the temple, but at night He went out and stayed on the mountain called Olivet. Then early in the morning all the people came to Him in the temple to hear Him" (Luke 21). So what was He doing on the mountain? That's where He often went to pray. Luke 22:39 says that it was His customary place of refuge. When Judas led his betrayal, he knew right where to find Jesus—the Mount of Olives. And what was Jesus doing there that evening? He was praying.

It's impossible to know what's on a man's heart if you never spend time with him, and so it is with God. Jesus knew the Father's heart. He knew the Father's will because He spent time in His Presence. Not in a legalistic, "I have to pray" kind of way. But rather in a, "I can't go without being near the One I love" kind of way. Martin Luther once said, "Prayer is the most important thing in my life. If I should neglect prayer for a single day, I should lose a great deal of the fire of my faith." It was John Wesley who said, "I have so much to do that I must spend several hours in prayer before I am able to do it."

When searching for God's will, nothing is more essential than prayer. Someone once said, "If you work for God, form a committee; if you work with God, form a prayer group." It's also important that we realize it's not the length of the prayer, but its depth that matters most. A short prayer will reach heaven quick if you don't live far away. Long prayers in public often indicate short prayers in private.

In Galatians 6, Paul says that following his conversation, he spent three years in the Arabian Desert. Before Jesus started His earthly ministry, that's where He went—the desert. Forty days of prayer and fasting prepared Him for three years of ministry that forever changed the history of mankind. In the words of John Maxwell, "When we work—we work, but when we pray—God works!" Prayer is the pause that empowers. What begins in prayer often ends in power. Satan laughs at our toil, mocks our wisdom, but trembles when we pray. A simple man on his knees can see far more than a king on his tiptoes. The truth is, God rules the world by the prayer of the saints. Sodom and Gomorrah were not destroyed because of their sin but because Abraham stopped praying. As long as Abraham petitioned God, mercy was extended. However, when he stopped interceding, judgment came upon the cities. In this life, nothing is as vital as prayer.

It's in prayer that God begins to reveal to us His wishes. Daniel said, "There is a God in heaven who reveals secrets . . ." (Daniel 2:28). Amos 3:7 says, "Surely the Lord GOD does nothing unless He reveals His secret to His servants the prophets." When's the last time God told you a secret? Begin to ask the Lord to increase your hunger for His Presence, to enlarge your craving for His fellowship, and to intensify your appetite for prayer. In his book, *Why Revival Tarries*, Leonard Ravenhill[2]* wrote: "No man is greater than his prayer life . . . We have many organizers, but few agonizers, many players and payers, few prayers. The ministry of preaching is open to a few, the ministry of prayer, the highest ministry of all human offices, is open to all."

A PIONEER'S JOURNAL:

If prayer is the most important Christian activity in which we take part, then it stands to reason that our enemy would do what he must to stop it. And maybe, among the greatest strategies to stop prayer would be to make prayer a most difficult and unattainable feat.

What are your conceptions about prayer, concerning the posture of prayer, concerning the repetition of prayer, concerning the length of prayer, concerning the words of prayer, concerning the silence of prayer?

---

2   *Leonard Ravenhill, *Why Revival Tarries* (Bloomington: Bethany House Publishers, 1979).

Is prayer about desire or is it an action necessary to earn God's blessing?

1 John 5:13–15 says this, "These things have I written unto you that believe on the name of the Son of God; that ye may know that ye have eternal life, and that ye may believe on the name of the Son of God. And this is the confidence that we have in him, that if we ask any thing according to his will, he hears us: And if we know that he hears us, whatsoever we ask, we know that we have the petitions that we desired of him."

"Asking according to His will" is the two million-dollar phrase! How can you be sure you are praying according to His will?

GOD'S WILL IN THREE CATEGORIES

Since the will of God is such a broad topic, let's view the subject from three different angles.

1. His sovereign will for what He has created
2. His moral will for all of us
3. His individual will for you and me

Firstly, understand that God has a sovereign will, a plan for what He has created, and nothing can prevent that from coming to pass—for example, the redemptive work of Christ. Nothing could hinder the birth, life, ministry, death, burial, and resurrection of Jesus. Even before the fall of man, the cross was God's sovereign plan. Christ was slain before the foundations of the earth. For thousands of years, Satan tried to prevent His coming. In the book of Exodus, Satan used Pharaoh. In the book of Esther, he used Haman. In the book of Matthew, Herod was the one used to thwart God's redemptive plan. Nothing can foil, put off, avert, inhibit, put a stop to, hinder, or get in the way of God's sovereign will for His creation. Nothing could prevent Jesus from coming the first time, nor will anything prevent Him from coming the second time. God's sovereign purpose is absolute and superior. It will not be tampered with or obstructed. So the first question is, "Where do we discover His sovereign will?" It's written in His Word. The more we study His Word, the more we understand His sovereign will.

Secondly, we know that God has a moral will—His desire concerning our conduct and behavior. In the Old Testament, we have the Ten Commandments. Fast forward into the New Testament and Jesus summed it all up with two commands: "Love God and love people." He dove even deeper during His Sermon on the Mount, saying things like, "You've heard it said, 'Do not murder,' but I say to you, 'Whoever's anger at his brother is without a cause is in danger of the judgment.'" We love to speak of grace and we all need it. But grace is not only the forgiveness of sin; it's also the empowerment to stop sinning. Our character is extremely important. Jesus said that we're known by the fruit we bear. 1 Peter 1:10 says, "But as He who called you is holy, you also be holy in all your conduct, because it is written, 'Be holy, for I am holy.' And if you call on the Father, who without partiality judges according to each one's work, conduct yourselves throughout the time of your stay here in fear . . ." In chapter two, verses eleven and twelve, Peter went on to say, "Dear friends, I urge you, as foreigners and exiles, to abstain from sinful desires, which wage war against your soul. Live such good lives among the pagans that, though they accuse you of doing wrong, they may see your good deeds and glorify God . . ."

Finally, we understand that God has a will or a plan for each individual person. As Miles Munroe said, "Purpose always precedes production." Nothing is made without a purpose. Everything created has an intended purpose. Everything begins with a purpose and ends with the product, and the product is always made perfect for its purpose.

Long before you became a reality, God thought you up. God looked down from heaven and saw a need in this world during this time, and His response to that need was you. Every day you wake up is a testimony that today the world needs you. You were fashioned for a purpose and you were created perfect for your purpose. God wired you for success. He spent much time planning and thinking before He began putting you together. Draftsmen make about 27,000 drawings for the manufacturing of a new car. God did more than that before He made you. We were never made to live and die without knowing why. So when searching for God's purpose for your life, remember, the more you understand His sovereign will, and the more you obey His moral will, the more you will find yourself living in the middle of His individual will for your life.

A PIONEER'S JOURNAL:

Form follows function is a principle associated with modern architecture and industrial design in the twentieth century. The principle is that the shape of a building or object should be primarily based upon its intended function or purpose. (Wikipedia) If function determines form, then your personality, your interests, your gifts, and your talents give insight as to where you fit into the scheme of your world.

What are some of your positive personality traits, your interests, your gifts, your talents? List them and ask the Holy Spirit for insight to embrace them so that you may function in them at the highest level of efficiency.

On a greater level, consider the masterpiece of the human form. Consider God's intent for its function.

THE POWER OF FASTING

Right before his fourth birthday, our son, Chaz, was diagnosed with Pervasive Developmental Disorder (PDD), which is on the autism spectrum. He said very little, mostly echoing what he heard others say. He was extremely introverted and avoided eye contact. There were some sensory issues as well. Cutting his hair, brushing his teeth, or trimming his nails was a major sensory overload. The neighbors probably thought we were killing him. And he hated when someone got in his space. I remember standing in the line at Chik-fil-A when a kid came right up in his face and tried to touch the toy in his hand. He freaked! And for some reason, he wrapped his arms around the waist of the dear old lady in front of us, stuck his nose right in her backside, shook his head from side to side, and screamed as loud as he could. The poor lady's knees buckled, and she fainted right then and there. Not really. Actually, she nearly jumped over the counter and looked at me like I had put him up to it. His preschool teachers told us that he "might" be able to attend a normal kindergarten classroom. Kindergarten came and went as did first grade. Toward the end of his second grade year, the diagnosis was removed and specialists at the University of Louisville told us that Chaz showed no signs associated with autism.

In the spring of 1993, Melissa was given only eight weeks to live. Ulcers in her colon had left her feebly malnourished and near death. Her doctor told her that unless she had her colon removed, she had no hope of surviving. At age twenty-three, she had reached her worst, weighing only seventy-eight pounds. Solid foods were too much for her troubled system, so for nearly a month, Melissa lived on popsicles and water, yet she still ran to the bathroom twenty or more times a day. But one night, all of that changed! God touched her body and within a few months, she was completely healed. Today, Melissa weighs 115 pounds and looks like a million bucks. And no, she never had her colon removed.

A common denominator in both these situations was prayer and fasting. For the first six years of Chaz's life, he never experienced a proper bowel moment. He would either go in his pants or in his sleep. We could not even get him to sit on a toilet without being frustrated. But on the seventh day of a liquid-only fast, I walked down the hall of our home and passed through a terrible smell coming from underneath the bathroom door. My boy was on the throne! I said, "Is that you in there, Chaz?" He said "Yep!" I said, "What are you doing?" With a little attitude in his voice he said, "I'm plop ploppin,' Daddy." He never again had a problem plop ploppin'. The Bible reveals to us the power of fasting (Matthew 17:21). Certain breakthroughs will come no other way.

Adam lost everything by eating. Jesus started everything by fasting. As Jentezen Franklin shares in his book on fasting,[3*] "When you eliminate food from your diet for a number of days, your spirit becomes amazingly sensitive to the things of God. If Jesus could have accomplished everything without fasting, then why did He fast? As David stated in Psalm 42, 'Deep calls unto deep.'" Going without food for a spiritual purpose is an undeniable way to experience spiritual breakthrough, not only in the area of healing, but also when it comes to seeking God's direction. Fasting heightens our sensitivity to God's voice. God says, "And you will seek Me and find Me, when you search for Me with all your heart" (Jeremiah 29:13). One of the first verses I memorized was 1 Corinthians 2:9: "But as it is written: Eye has not seen, nor ear heard, nor have entered into the heart of man the things which God has prepared for those who love Him." Unfortunately, ten years passed before I paid any attention to the verse that follows

---

3   · Jentezen Franklin, *Fasting* (Gainesville, GA: Jentezen Franklin Ministries, 2004) p. 21.

it. In verse ten, Paul went on to say, "But God has revealed them to us through His Spirit. For the Spirit searches all things, yes, the deep things of God." When I fast, I send my spirit in search of the deep things of God. Again, some things can only be discovered through fasting.

Let's look at a few examples of how fasting was used in Scripture. As the exiled Jews prepared to return to Jerusalem, Ezra called for a national fast. "Then I proclaimed a fast there at the river of Ahava, that we might humble ourselves before our God, to seek from Him the right way for us and our little ones and all our possessions. For I was ashamed to request of the king an escort of soldiers and horsemen to help us against the enemy on the road, because we had spoken to the king, saying, 'The hand of our God *is* upon all those for good who seek Him, but His power and His wrath *are* against all those who forsake Him.' So we fasted and entreated our God for this, and He answered our prayer . . . Then we departed from the river of Ahava on the twelfth *day* of the first month, to go to Jerusalem. And the hand of our God was upon us, and He delivered us from the hand of the enemy and from ambush along the road" (Ezra 8:21–23, 31).

When Nehemiah heard of the destruction of Jerusalem, he sat down and wept. With his face to the ground, he prayed and fasted for several days (Nehemiah 1:4). He spent four months in prayer before he made his request to the king (Nehemiah 1:1, 2:1). God honored his brokenness by moving on the heart of King Artaxerxes, king of Persia. Under the king's command, Nehemiah was commissioned to rebuild the walls of Jerusalem. Underwriting the project was the king himself. Nehemiah came as civil governor, with authority from the king of Persia to refortify the battered city.

Once Esther caught wind of Haman's plan to destroy the Jews, her initial reaction was to call a fast. Haman's plan was spoiled and in the end, he hung from the gallows he had built for Esther and her people. Michael, the archangel, was released the moment Daniel began to fast. One of the most intense spiritual battles mentioned in the Old Testament was the result of one man's fast.

After Paul met the Lord on the road to Damascus, he embarked on a three-day fast (Acts 9:9). In Acts 10:30, we discover that Cornelius was four days into a fast and the Holy Spirit was poured out upon the Gentiles. When the apostles ordained elders in the church, prayer and fasting accompanied their decisions (Acts 14:23). Job said that he treasured the words from God's mouth more than he did his necessary food (Job 23:12).

A PIONEER'S JOURNAL:

Is fasting a right, a privilege, or a duty?

Reference Isaiah 58. Sometimes it's easier to go without food than to go without self-centeredness. Using this scriptural reference, make a list of what God desires from His people in a fast.

BEFORE YOU GO . . .

If you're doing something for God, it's a guaranteed success. At least that's what I used to think. But after wrecking four church buses, I had to re-evaluate all that.

When our family announced that we were moving to Atlanta to plant a new church, I recall someone asking, "What will you do if it doesn't work out?" I thought, *Not work out? How could God stuff not work out?* Doesn't the Bible say, "If God be for me who can be against me?" (Romans 8:31). What about, "I can do all things through Christ who strengthens me" (Philippians 4:13) or "With God all things are possible"? (Matthew 19:26). I could go on and on with biblical promises to assure my success. I was convinced that if something was God's will, it would come together with ease. Unfortunately, that hasn't always been my story.

Have you ever heard of Billy Herman?

He had a successful baseball career, playing in the big league for two decades. But his career didn't start off so well.

It was his first time to bat playing with the big boys. The Cubs' new second baseman stepped to the plate and fouled the ball. The ball hit the dirt, ricocheted back up, hit him in the head, and knocked him out cold. Herman was carried off the field on a stretcher.

I have a friend who has planted hundreds of churches and mentored many great men and women of God. He once told me that during his first Sunday as a young pastor, a woman died on the front pew (during his preaching). Whether it's true or not I'm not sure, but I once heard that in preparation to launch their company, FedEx shipped two packages—neither of them arrived at their destination.

What's the difference between a failure and success?

The answer is simply: one more try.

People don't fail; they give up.

So whatever God's put in your heart—go for it! Don't give up. Don't throw in the towel. As Habakkuk 2:3 says, "Though it tarries, wait for it; because it will surely come . . ." Let me end our time together by saying a prayer for you.

"Lord, thank You for creating my dear friend. I thank You for the plans You have for them. Blow their mind with Your incredible love, grace, power, vision, revelation, provision, and favor. Your word says that You will perfect those things which concern us and that You will finish the good work that You have begun in us. Goodness and mercy shall follow us all the days of our lives. We will be like trees planted by the rivers of water, we will bring forth fruit in our season, our leaves shall not wither, and whatsoever we do shall prosper. Thank You for bringing those things to pass in the life of my friend reading this book right now. Amen!"

ABOUT THE AUTHOR

Jason Creech became a Jesus follower at age 19. After earning his bachelor's degree in art and design, he took his first staff position at a local church in Southeastern Kentucky. He has 14 years of pastoral experience in the area of student ministry. In 2006, Jason founded Mirror-Mirror, a nonprofit organization that allowed him to bring high-energy events, college scholarships, cash prizes, and the hope found in Jesus Christ to over 58,000 public school students throughout Kentucky and abroad.

OUR FAMILY

Dealing with the S-Words by Jason Creech

Rich or poor, popular or unnoticed, we're all looking for the same thing—new life. But if young people don't get things right on the inside, they will never be the happy, successful people they were created to be. Happiness and success are an inside job. This is a book about "S-Words"—the "don't go there" words—those topics that get Sunday school teachers replaced and youth pastors fired: self-esteem, significance, sex, secrets, and suicide. Dive deeply into the topics we've all wrestled with and discover what God says about life's toughest issues.

new.u by Jason Creech

Are you just getting started as a new Christian? Then you probably have a lot of questions. In this five-week devotional, you'll discover a boatload of answers. Learn the simplicity of the Christian life. Welcome to freedom. Welcome to the new u.

Check out these additional titles by
Innovo Publishing.

Order online at
www.innovopublishing.com.

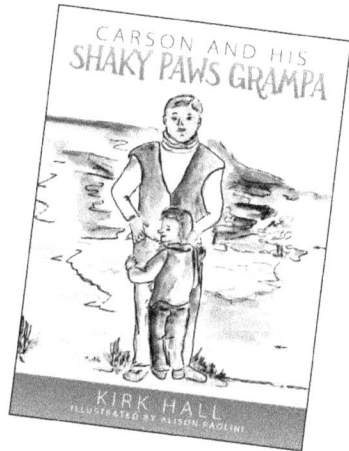

Blinders, a novel by Kristy Shelton, portrays a beautiful relationship between a former slave couple, their love for a boy who wanders onto their farm, and the redeeming forgiveness of the heavenly Father. In this inspirational novel, Eugene, an eleven-year-old boy growing up in Kentucky in 1912, is led to the farm of Franklin and Rachel Hawkins. Eugene is adopted into the family and gradually discovers secrets from the past that keep Franklin and Rachel isolated on their remote farm. Eugene is severely tested when he is seized from the farm at the age of sixteen and forced into the Great War. He embarks on a dangerous journey that will put his life and faith to the test.

Carson and His Shaky Paws Grampa by Kirk Hall, is a story about the relationship and love between a grandfather who has Parkinson's disease and his seven-year-old grandson. The story is designed to help parents and grandparents comfortably talk about the initial symptoms of Parkinson's and address common questions and concerns children may express. A portion of the proceeds from every sale will be donated to Parkinson's research.

ABOUT INNOVO PUBLISHING

Innovo Publishing is a full-service Christian publisher serving the Christian and wholesome markets. Innovo creates, distributes, and markets quality hardback and paperback books, eBooks (Kindle, Nook, iPhone, iPad, ePub), audiobooks and music (CDs and MP3s), and videos through traditional publishing, cooperative publishing, and independent publishing models. Innovo provides distribution, marketing, and automated order fulfillment through a network of thousands of physical and online wholesalers, retailers, bookstores, music stores, schools, and libraries worldwide including Amazon, Audible, iTunes, Rhapsody, Barnes & Noble, and many more. Innovo publishes Christian fiction and non-fiction books and wholesome books for all publishing genres. Visit Innovo at www.innovopublishing.com.

innovo
PUBLISHING

FOR A HIGHER PURPOSE

www.ingramcontent.com/pod-product-compliance
Lightning Source LLC
Chambersburg PA
CBHW031857090426
42741CB00005B/537